ontents (Third Edition)

G000167610

The East Berkshire RA Group was formed in 1970 to protect and restore to good order all the public rights of way in this part of Berkshire, and also to seek improvements to the existing footpath network. The Group endeavours to keep under regular surveillance all 1200 paths in the area and will take up irregularities with parish councils, district councils and the County Council to preserve public rights.

Working parties of Group members have cleared over 48 miles of overgrown paths, erected or repaired 605 signposts, built or repaired 220 stiles and 86 footbridges. Regular walks are held, to which newcomers are always welcome, to encourage the use of paths and enjoyment of the countryside. For further details of the Group please contact the Membership Secretary:
Rita North, 14 Gossmore Walk, Gossmore Lane, Marlow, Bucks. SL7 1QZ

Roman Walk and Loddon Drive

distance 4 mile

This circular walk, of just over four miles in length (made possible by a permitted path at Loddon Park Farm), after leaving the riverside village of Wargrave, is largely through the green meadows that adjoin the River Loddon.

The directions below start from the car park in School Lane, Wargrave (Grid Ref. 786786), but the map of the route may suggest other starting places (e.g. Wargrave Station). For further topographical features of the area, see the Ordnance Survey Pathfinder map 1172 'Reading'. Please observe the Country Code; in particular, keep to footpaths, keep dogs on lead across farmland and leave all wild flowers for others to enjoy.

From car park, turn right down School Lane to crossroads, here cross over and turn left along main road (A321) using footway in front of the 'Bull Hotel'. After about 200 yards, at the 'Old Mill House', turn right into Station Road, then immediately after 'The Vicarage' on left, turn left into narrow raised woodland strip - Roman Walk.

Emerging at bend in tarmac road, continue straight on along road passing over Western Region Henley branch line (opened 1857) and on reaching entrance to sewage works, fork left to follow edge of field (a permitted path) with wire fence on right. After end of sewage works, still keep to field edge, but bear left and remain in same field with ditch on right, then on reaching solitary white house 'Riverways' ahead, turn half left along gravel track to reach Bath Road (A4).

Turn right along tarmac footway and about 125 yards after crossing the second of two bridges over the twin branches of the River Loddon, turn right into winding hedged and fenced tarmac track - Loddon Drive - a private road but a public footpath. In 1981 there was an application to extract sand and gravel from these meadows, but it was refused on appeal as it would cause significant harm to this Thames Valley area of special landscape character.

After just over three-quarters of a mile along track, cross steel bridge over St. Patrick's Stream, but here pause for vie across meadows ahead, of white painte Shiplake House, red-brick Shiplake College and the Parish Church of St. Peter and St. Paul overlooking the River Thames. Now bear right to continue or fenced gravel track and shortly after the red brick Borough Bridge, keep straight on along gravel drive.

Follow drive through left-hand bend at property 'Cherry Eyot' and after nearly half-a-mile, at crossing tarmac track, turr right and in about 60 yards cross River Loddon again by the metal and concrete Bridgeman's Bridge. Continue ahead on winding tarmac drive, pass through brick tunnel under railway and follow road to the right, next to railway embankment, to reach junction at approach to Wargrave Station, here turn left along Station Road.

Near far end of road, just before 'Give Way' sign, turn left on tarmac path along edge of green. To the left is the attractive flint and brick parish church of St. Mary's, rebuilt in 1916 after being almost completely destroyed by fire on the night of June 1, 1914. The War Memorial on the green was designed by Sir Edwin Lutyens.

In far corner of green, pass through metal swing gate and continue along road (Church Street) for about 25 yards - here keep straight on to continue the walk, or turn left into Ferry Lane and shortly left again (opposite Ferry Cottage) down gravel track, for access to the River Thames at the Parish Council's landing stage for light craft.

In Church Street, note on left the Woodclyffe Hostel, presented by the late Mrs. Harriet Cook Smith in March 1906; it was erected on the site of Queen Emma's Palace (Queen Emma was the wife of Ethelred and Canute and mother of Edward the Confessor). Finally, at traffic lights ahead, cross over into School Lane to return to car park at start.

DATE WALKED [   ][19   ]

Ramble No. 1

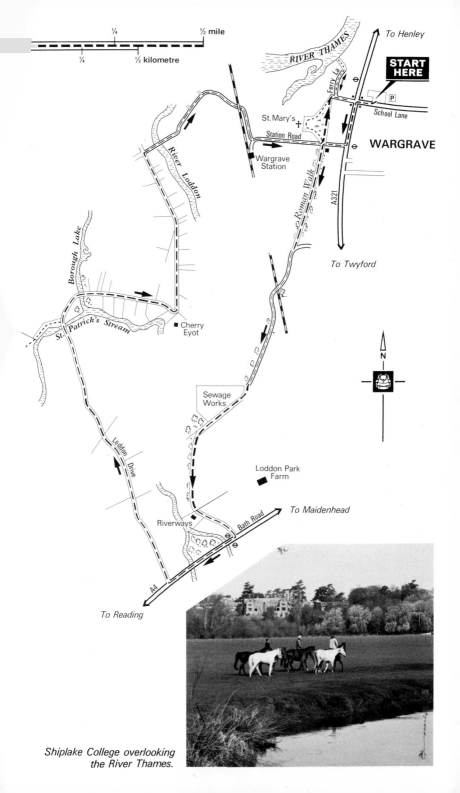

¼ mile

¼   ½ kilometre

RIVER THAMES

To Henley

START HERE

P

Ferry la.

River Loddon

St. Mary's

Station Road

WARGRAVE

School Lane

Wargrave Station

Roman Walk

A321

To Twyford

Borough Lake

St. Patrick's Stream

■ Cherry Eyot

N

Sewage Works

Loddon Park Farm

Loddon Drive

To Maidenhead

Riverways

Bath Road

A4

To Reading

Shiplake College overlooking the River Thames.

Binfield Heath and Shiplake Woods

distance 3¹/₄ or 4 mile

This circular walk, of about 4 miles in length, is through the quiet and pleasant farmland and woodland to the west of Shiplake. Within the route is described a shorter alternative of 3¹/₄ miles.

The directions below start from the Recreation Ground (limited parking) at Binfield Heath (Grid Ref. 746786), but the map of the route may suggest other starting places. For further topographical features of the area, see the Ordnance Survey Pathfinder map 1172 'Reading'. Please observe the Country Code; in particular, keep to footpaths, keep dogs on lead across farmland and leave all wild flowers for others to enjoy.

With your back to entrance to Recreation Ground, turn right along road and shortly at Post Office, fork left along unmade road, Heathfield Avenue. Just after first pair of red brick cottages on left, fork left into fenced and hedged tarmac path to reach gravel track ahead. Now continue straight on and shortly enter field by stile, then go half right through middle of field to hedge at side of field, here bear left to follow edge of field keeping hedge on right. Pass into next field through gap in hedge and at bottom of descent enter woodland strip over stile ahead. After stile at top of climb, keep straight on through middle of field to stile into High Wood, here continue ahead on waymarked (painted white arrows) woodland path.

Emerging from woodland, keep straight on along gravel track with fence of paddock on right, then after kink in track, pass 'Upper Bolney House' on right and continue on concrete road. Where road bends left, at property 'Little Spinneys', turn sharp right through gateway and through middle of field, passing under power lines, to reach right-hand end of woodland ahead - Shiplake Woods, part of the Forestry Commission's Chiltern Forest.

Continue ahead along track and on emerging from woods to follow broad grassy track, look left along here for distant views of Bowsey Hill on far side of Thames Valley. At junction with broad track turn right along it for about 200 yards to a bungalow, here turn left and follow edge of field with hedge on right to road ahead. Cross over road to near corner of 'The White Hart' car park here is the choice of route.

The 4 mile walk passes to left of 'The White Hart', but for the 3¹/₄ mile walk continue along road past the pub for about 100 yards, then turn right up steps to follow path along top of bank parallel with road. Rejoin road shortly before field entrance. After about 300 yards along road, immediately before red tiled and white painted property 'Dormons', turn right over stile and along edge of small field. After stile ahead, turn half left though middle of field to another stile to right of large tree, here pass in front of two red brick bungalows and continue on gravel track to return to start.

To continue the 4 mile walk, pass through gap in hedge of car park and continue through middle of field to double power line poles at left-hand end of copse. Now turn half right with copse on right to next power line pole, here turn half right up through middle of field. After crossing grass track, keep straight on with field boundary nearby on right to enter Shiplake Copse in far right-hand corner. Entering woodland, bear slightly right to follow gently climbing path, then move up bank on right, to follow edge of two fields (divided by iron 'kissing gate') with hedge and trees on left. At road ahead, turn right along road and when in sight of road junction at Binfield Heath, at metal barrier on left, enter other entrance to Recreation Ground and turn right across grass to return to start.

DATE WALKED ☐ ☐ 19 ☐

Ramble No. 2

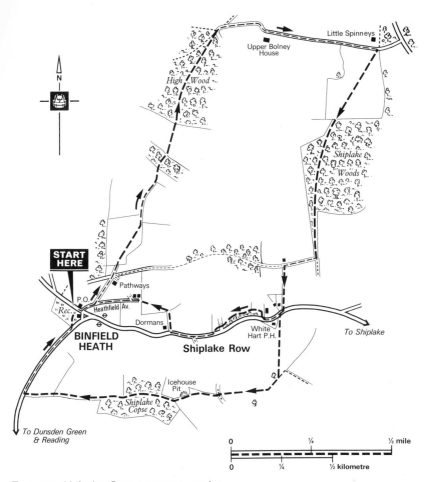

N

START HERE

High Wood

Upper Bolney House

Little Spinneys

Shiplake Woods

Pathways

P.O.

Rec.

Heathfield Av.

Dormans

BINFIELD HEATH

Shiplake Row

White Hart P.H.

To Shiplake

Icehouse Pit

Shiplake Copse

To Dunsden Green & Reading

| 0 | ¼ | ½ mile |
| 0 | ¼ | ½ kilometre |

Two year old Amber Parry, youngest member of the East Berkshire RA Group, enjoying a ramble with her parents.   Photo: D.J.Ward

Morgans Wood and Crowsley Park

distance 3 mile[s]

This short circular walk, of just 3 miles in length, to the east of Sonning Common, is through some very pleasant Chiltern countryside and attractive parkland.

The directions below start from a point (Grid Ref. 719790) about 1/4 mile down the lane to Dunsden Green from 'Bird in Hand' on B481, where verge is wide enough for limited parking (do not obstruct field entrance), but the map of the route may suggest other starting places or alternative walks. For further topographical features of the area, see the Ordnance Survey Pathfinder maps 1172 'Reading' and 1156 'Henley-on-Thames'. Please observe the Country Code; in particular, keep to footpaths, keep dogs on lead across farmland and leave all wild flowers for others to enjoy.

Facing Dunsden Green direction, continue along lane for about 200 yards to stile on left, just before two cottages ahead, here turn left through middle of field (passing under power lines) to centre of woodland ahead - Morgan's Wood.

Enter woods by stile and follow waymarked (painted white arrows) path ahead to soon have fence and field on right. Emerge from woods by stile to keep along edge of field with fence and hedge on right, and after a further stile, continue on grass and then gravel track past 'The Well House' on right. Shortly, at thatched 'Frieze Cottage', turn right along narrow road for just over 1/4 mile and at road junction ahead, turn left along road. After about 150 yards, turn right through gateway, past Lodge on right, into Crowsley Park - a property in the ownership of the British Broadcasting Corporation used as a receiving station.

Keep along tarmac drive and when opposite mansion on right, turn right over stile and in about 100 yards cross a further stile into parkland. Maintain same direction through middle of parkland to another stile, just to left of group of four large trees (two are hidden). Then continue straight on across open parkland for about 250 yards towards single large conifer, a few yards beyond which turn sharp right on defined straight grass path. Cross avenue of oaks (leading to house on right), drawing closer to fence and trees on right, to leave parkland by stile in far corner. Descending brick steps, cross road to stile opposite and continue ahead across corner of field to another stile, here turn right along gravel track towards buildings of Crowsley Park Farm.

At end of farm buildings on right, bear left over stile and continue along edge of field with fence on right. In corner of this field turn left to still follow hedge on right, now steeply downhill. About half-way up slope ahead cross two stiles in hedge on right. In next field continue along headland (field edge) with hedge on left and in far corner, enter next field at opening and turn right along edge of field with hedge on right. At end of field pass over stile and at end of access track to red brick cottages on left, turn right along lane to return to parking place at start.

DATE WALKED [   ] 19

Ramble No. 3

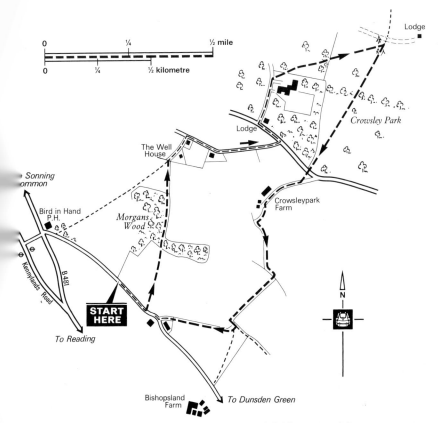

Follow path through Morgan's Wood with fence and field on your right.

Peppard Common and Kidmore End

distance 7½ mile

This circular walk, of about 7½ miles in length, is through gently undulating typical Chiltern countryside and does a complete circuit of Sonning Common.

The directions below start from the Recreation Ground car park (behind tennis court) adjacent to Bishopswood School, Sonning Common (Grid Ref. 698807), but the map of the route should suggest other starting places. For further topographical features of the area, see the Ordnance Survey Pathfinder maps 1172 'Reading' and 1156 'Henley-on-Thames'. Please observe the Country Code.

Leaving car park, turn right along Horsepond Road for about 125 yards, then turn left into gravel track. Pass through gap next to gate and after a further 50 yards, climb stile on right and go half left through middle of field towards near end of hedge dividing two distant fields. Pass over stile in far boundary and continue along edge of next two fields with tall hedge on left to reach road (Wyfold Lane) after stile, here turn right along road, passing former hospital nearby on left. Cross over at road ahead and bear right to follow lane to the right of 'The Unicorn', then between properties 'Clare House' and 'Manor View', enter up steps on right, path between metal railings. Follow winding path between cottages to emerge on the edge of Peppard Common.

Continue on broad woodland track ahead, then when this track starts to curve tightly right, turn very sharp left down woodland path. At bottom of descent turn right along broad grass path and at clearing at end, turn left up steep narrow winding woodland path (with main road nearby on right) to reach road on edge of open common, here turn right along road. Shortly cross over road ahead and keep straight on across grass to enter and follow Church Lane to the right of Peppard Primary School. Passing the flint-faced All Saints Church (largely rebuilt around 1875) on left, continue on gravel track

and in front of 'Rectory Cottage', turn right for about 20 yards to stile, then turn left along edge of field with cottag on left.

Follow right hand-bend at end of field and in next corner turn left through woodland strip. In next field, turn right and then left along edge of field, to reach buildings of Bottom Barn, here turn right up broad hedged track. Keep left at Blounts Farm and shortly turn left along road, then near end of copse on left, turn right up steps and through middle of field. At large tree at near corner of long garden turn left along edge of same field with trees on right. At power line pole, turn right along edge of small field with fence on left to reach road (Blackmore Lane) at 'Pond Farm Cottage', here turn left down this narrow lane. At junction ahead, turn right along road for about ¼ mile, then turn right along lane towards Frieze Farm and after following lane through left-hand bend, immediately before the thatched 'Frieze Cottage', turn right into gravel track.

Enter grass path to right of 'Well House' and after stile continue through middle of field to right-hand end of woodland ahead, here after stile, maintain same direction through middle of next two fields to reach road just after stile. Now turn right along road, with care cross over main road (B481) at 'Bird in Hand' to pass through metal swing gate opposite, then go half right through middle of field and after crossing road (Kennylands Road) ahead, enter path to right of property 'Winters Folly'. At end of this fenced path, bear slightly right along broad fenced grass path and after metal rails continue in same direction through middle of next field. Pass through woodland strip ahead and keep along edge of next field with fence on left, then after stile next to white farm gate, turn right along narrow tarmac road. Passing to left of Vines Farm continue on hedged track and immediately after the white 'Emmens Cottage', turn left over stile and through middle of

continued on next page

Ramble No. 4

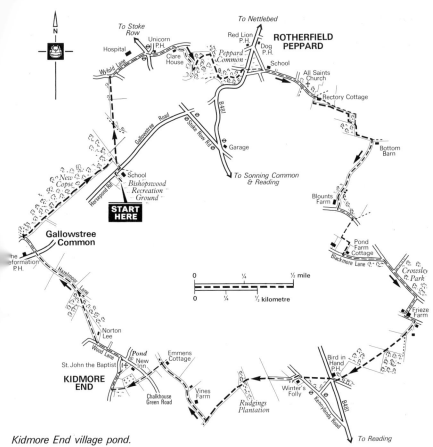

To Nettlebed

N

To Stoke Row

Hospital

Unicorn P.H.

Clare House

Wytold Lane

Red Lion P.H.

Peppard Common

Dog P.H.

ROTHERFIELD PEPPARD

School

All Saints Church

Rectory Cottage

B481

Gallowstree Road

Stoke Row Rd

Garage

To Sonning Common & Reading

Bottom Barn

School

Horsepond Rd

Bishopswood Recreation Ground

START HERE

Blounts Farm

Pond Farm Cottage

Blackmore Lane

New Copse

Gallowstree Common

Crowsley Park

The Reformation P.H.

Hazelmoor Lane

0 ¼ ½ mile

0 ¼ ½ kilometre

Frieze Farm

Norton Lee

Wood Lane

Pond New Inn

Emmens Cottage

St. John the Baptist

KIDMORE END

Chalkhouse Green Road

Vines Farm

Rudgings Plantation

Winter's Folly

Bird in Hand P.H.

Kennylands Road

B481

To Reading

Kidmore End village pond.

field to shortly enter fenced path leading to road (Chalkhouse Green Road) at Kidmore End. Cross over into Coopers Pightle, continue along edge of cemetery and Recreation Ground, and at road ahead, turn right to soon pass through churchyard of the flint-faced St. John the Baptist (consecrated in 1852) on right. At road junction, by old well, go left along Wood Lane to continue walk, but it is worth going right for about 50 yards to visit the village pond. Just before bend in road, fork right by property 'Norton Lee' into fenced path and after passing through woodland ahead, turn left along tarmac lane (Hazelmoor Lane). At junction at Gallowstree Common, cross over into road opposite and at bend in road, turn sharp right through stileway to follow path along edge of woods. At end of woods, turn right along track and at road ahead, turn right past school to return to car park at start.

DATE WALKED [ ] [19]

Withy Copse and Deadman's Lane

distance 4½ mile

This mostly flat circular walk, of about 4½ miles in length, explores the beautiful beechwoods around Cane End, a hamlet situated 4 miles north west of Reading.

The directions below start from the small lane (limited parking on verge) on the east side of 'The Fox Inn', Cane End (Grid Ref. 680795), but the map of the route may suggest other starting places (e.g. Park Lane) or shorter alternatives. For further topographical features of the area, see the Ordnance Survey Pathfinder maps 1172 'Reading' and 1156 'Henley-on-Thames'. Please observe the Country Code; in particular, keep to footpaths, keep dogs on lead across farmland and leave all wild flowers for others to enjoy.

Facing main road (A4074), turn right along road on grass verge passing 'The Fox Inn' on right, cross over the end of Horsepond Road and immediately after white thatched 'Well Cottage' turn right along tarmac drive. In about 50 yards, at entrance to property 'Clervaux', pass over stile into field on left and continue along edge of field with hedge on right to stile at road (Park Lane), here turn left along road. At bungalow on right, turn right through wooden gate between bungalow and garage across lawn to enter woods ahead, then bear left on waymarked (painted white arrows) woodland path, with conifer plantation at first on left, through Withy Copse.

On reaching far side of woodland, turn right along curved track just inside woods to meet at top of rise ahead, road opposite 'Kates Cottage', here turn left along road passing site of one-time fort (Castle Grove) on right. At end of field on left, turn left into track along edge of woodland with large field on left. On eventually reaching road ahead (Park Lane), turn right along road for about 15 yards, then turn left along edge of field with hedge on left. After passing isolated cottage on left, continue ahead, on tarmac then concrete road and at junction ahead, with care cross over (A4074) into road opposite (B4526) -

Deadman's Lane.

Keeping to verge on right follow road for nearly ½ mile, then about 30 yards after 'slow' sign painted on road, turn left along edge of woods with birch plantation and then fields nearby on left. At end of second field keep straight on through woodland to soon have long thin field nearby on left and after emerging from woodland along hedged path, bear slightly right along gravel track. At bend in track ahead at the hamlet of Nuney Green, immediately before bungalow 'Cross Ways' on right, turn left into woods on waymarked woodland path to eventually follow track along edge of woods with field on right, forking right at pit ahead.

Emerge from woodland by slightly sunken path then, on reaching field ahead, turn left over stile and continue up through middle of field to stile at right-hand end of copse on horizon. Maintain same direction through middle of next field to stile near far end of fence on left. After stile maintain same direction to reach shortly road (A4074) after stile next to gate, here with care cross road to return to start.

DATE WALKED   19

Ramble No. 5

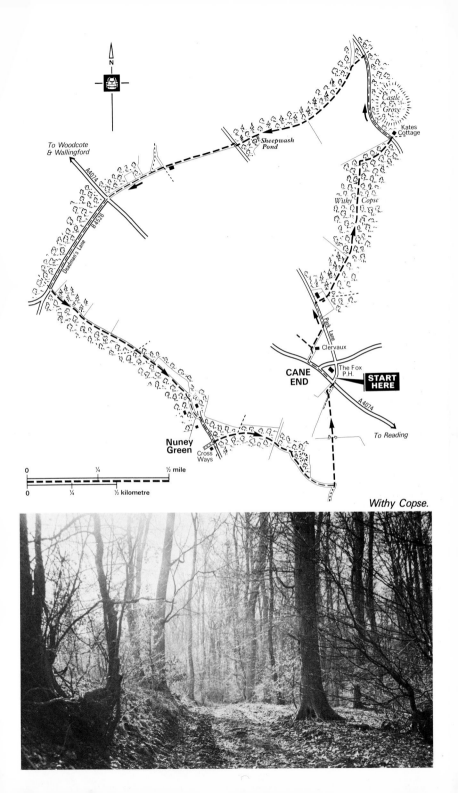

To Woodcote
& Wallingford

A4074

Dead man's Lane

B4526

Sheepwash
Pond

Castle
Grove

Kates
Cottage

Withy
Copse

Clervaux

Park Lane

The Fox
P.H.

CANE
END

START
HERE

A4074

To Reading

Nuney
Green

Cross
Ways

N

| 0 | ¼ | ½ mile |

| 0 | ¼ | ½ kilometre |

Withy Copse.

Whittles Farm and Collins End

This circular walk, of about 5 miles in length, passes through the quiet beech-woods around the hamlet of Nuney Green, descends steeply to the peaceful and attractive small riverside village of Mapledurham, then returns to Goring Heath up through the beeches of Bottom Wood and across the open green of Collins End.

The directions below start from the post office at Goring Heath (Grid Ref. 657792), but the map of the route may suggest other starting places or shorter alternatives. For further topographical features of the area see the Ordnance Survey Pathfinder map 1172 'Reading'. Please observe the Country Code; in particular, keep to footpaths, keep dogs on lead across farmland and leave all wild flowers for others to enjoy.

With post office on your right, cross into road (Deadman's Lane) ahead and after about 100 yards along road, fork right through metal gate along hedged track, and after about 120 yards enter field on right over stile. Follow field edge around property (Haw Farm) and at far side cross stile. Go ahead into large field, pass just to left of power line pole, and follow field edge to enter woods ahead over stile. Continue ahead on waymarked (painted white arrows) woodland path and at far side of woods pass over stile and keep on through middle of further woodland ahead.

Leave this woodland by stile and continue along edge of field with fence and trees on right to reach road by stile next to metal gate, here with care turn right along road, keeping to verge on right for about 200 yards, then turn right over stile. Follow edge of small field ahead with hedge on left to enter vine-yard through narrow metal gate. Continue straight on to leave vineyard by similar gate just to left of large oak tree, here bear slightly right through middle of field to stile at kink in far woodland boundary. Just inside woods, turn right along woodland path and at path junction ahead, at the hamlet Nuney Green, turn left along gravel track

for about 40 yards past the bungalow 'Cross Ways' then fork right into hedged path and, after conifers on right, enter woodland path ahead. Shortly after field appears on left, leave woodland by stile and continue straight on between trees on left and fence on right to reach road after stile, here cross road into tarmac track opposite leading to Whittles Farm.

After farm buildings on right, continue on farm track to where it turns left, here turn right over stile and along edge of field with fence and trees on left and fine views ahead over Mapledurham and the Thames Valley. After stile next to metal gate, continue steeply downhill on broad grass track to reach valley bottom, here turn left along track and then concrete road through the buildings of Bottom Farm. At bend in road ahead, bear right along road and at first property on right 'The White House' turn right along track to continue walk - or keep along road if you wish to visit the picturesque Thameside village of Mapledurham (no direct access to river) with its attractive flint and brick parish church of St. Margaret's. Mapledurham House and Mill (the oldest mill on the Thames) are open to the public at weekends during the summer (see Ramble No. 8). 'The White House' was once the village inn until closed by the Lord of the Manor in Victorian times.

Now follow gently climbing fenced track for about 1/2 mile, then on approaching house in trees (lodge to Hardwick Park) ahead, turn right over stile and bear left very steeply uphill to enter by stile at top, Bottom Wood. Continue ahead on gently descending waymarked wood-land path, keeping straight on after crossing shallow valley and then climb to eventually reach tarmac road after passing between white buildings. Now follow this road through Collins End, then where road bends right, keep straight on into tree lined path to reach road ahead and to return to start.

DATE WALKED [   ][   ] 19 [   ]

Ramble No. 6

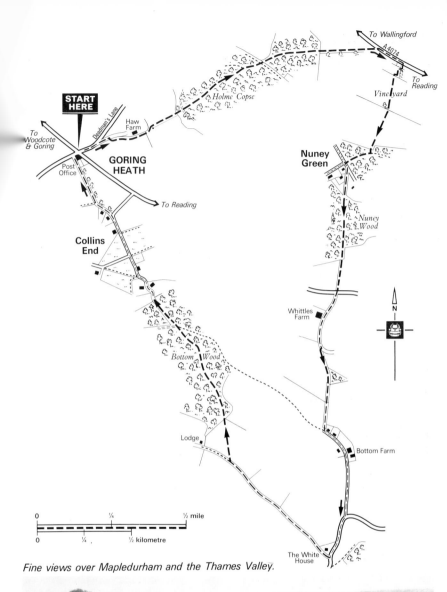

START HERE

To Wallingford

A4074

To Reading

Deadman's Lane

Holme Copse

Vineyard

To Woodcote & Goring

Haw Farm

GORING HEATH

Post Office

To Reading

Nuney Green

Nuney Wood

Collins End

Whittles Farm

Bottom Wood

N

Lodge

Bottom Farm

The White House

0		¼		½ mile

0		¼		½ kilometre

Fine views over Mapledurham and the Thames Valley.

Westbury Farm and Sulham Woods

distance 5 mile

This circular walk, of about 5 miles in length, through the rolling hills and flat meadows between Tilehurst and Pangbourne, provides some magnificent views of the Chiltern Hills across the Thames Valley. The route also includes optional visits to the Thames and the River Pang, but these will add about an extra mile to the walk.

The directions below start from near the south end of Long Lane, Purley (Grid Ref. 656746) where there is ample verge for parking, but the map of the route may suggest other starting places. For further topographical features of the area, see the Ordnance Survey Pathfinder map 1172 'Reading'. Please observe the Country Code; in particular, keep to footpaths, and keep dogs on lead across farmland.

From the north side of Vicarage Wood, with your back to field and road, climb stile next to metal gate to follow gravel track and shortly enter field ahead. Keep to field track with trees on right, then just after last tree, at path junction, continue ahead on well-defined path through middle of large field. At far boundary, continue along edge of next field to end of wood on left, here bear left through middle of field for about 70 yards, then turn right in direction of clump of tall trees at near end of woodland strip on right. Keep straight on through middle of woodland strip ahead, then at far end, about half way down edge of field, turn right over stile and shortly bear right along Beech Road. Immediately after No.34, just before more recent properties ahead, turn left down fenced gravel path and with care cross over main road (A329) ahead.

Now turn right along road and about 40 yards BEFORE roundabout turn left down broad gravel track and then concrete road to cross bridge over railway. On far side, turn left into fenced path to follow railway in cutting on left and at bridge ahead, turn right along tarmac road. Then, immediately after pair of red brick and tile cottages on left, at entrance to Springs Farm, turn left to

continue on tarmac road. After 'cottages' on right, continue ahead along broad fenced track, gravel at first, then grass. At end of fence on left, turn half left through middle of field to near side of tunnel, here keep along edge of same field with railway embankment on left. At end of field, turn left to continue walk - or turn right along well defined grass path on near side of stream, to visit banks of the River Thames opposite the Hardwick House estate.

Following concrete road right after tunnel, shortly turn left along edge of field with stream on right, then at main road (A329) ahead, with care cross over and turn right along footway. Immediately before garage on left, turn left into tarmac path 'Chiltern Walk', then after passing front gardens of Nos. 10 to 7, turn right to pass in front of Nos. 6 to 1, to reach road ahead. Now turn right along road, then shortly turn left between Nos. 24 and 10 to reach stile and then wooden swing gate, here turn right along edge of field with a fence on right. At wooden footbridge on left, turn left across it and through middle of field to continue walk - or keep straight on and through next field, to visit banks of River Pang at a footbridge.

Near far side of field, cross over another footbridge, to soon reach white foot-bridge and stile at boundary, here keep straight on through middle of next field. After stile ahead, turn right along road (Sulham Lane) and about 150yards after Lodge on left, turn left over stile and up through middle of field to stile into the Forestry Commission's Sulham Woods. Continue ahead on steeply climbing woodland path, keep straight on through middle of conifer plantation and on emerging from trees, continue along edge of field with fence on right. After stile at far boundary, bear right on well-defined path through middle of large field to wooden post at path junction, at highest point, here turn right with trees on left to return to start.

Ramble No. 7

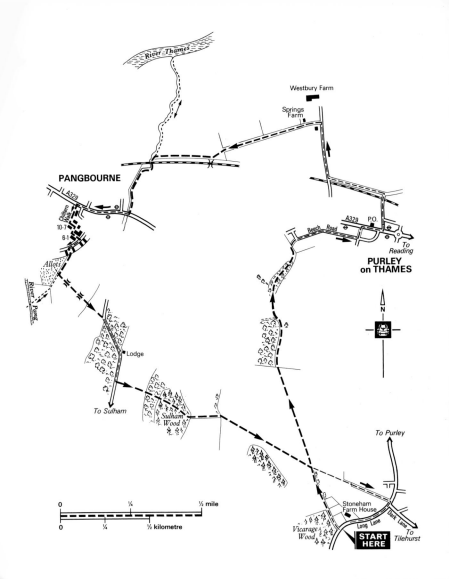

Publications

Footpath Maps

Rambling for Pleasure

Each illustrated booklet contains at least twenty short circular walks.

All these publications, including this booklet, are available from local bookshops and stationers or by post 35p extra (cheques made payable to E.Berks RA Group) from:
Pat Hayers, 16 Lanterns Walk, Farthingales, Maidenhead, Berkshire SL6 1TG

Newell's Lane and Chazey Wood

distance 1½ or 4¾ mile

This circular walk, of about 4¾ miles in length, is through pleasant rolling countryside on the edge of the Thames Valley between Caversham and Mapledurham. Within the route is described a shorter alternative of just over 1½ miles.

The directions below start from the old road (where there is limited parking at both ends) leading to the 'Pack Saddle' public house, Chazey Heath (Grid Ref. 695772), but the map of the route may suggest other shorter alternative walks. For further topographical features of the area, see the Ordnance Survey Pathfinder map 1172 'Reading'. Please observe the Country Code; in particular, keep to footpaths, keep dogs on lead across farmland and leave all wild flowers for others to enjoy.

From north end of old road, with your back to the 'Pack Saddle', go ahead along footway on right of A4074, then about 25 yards after Rokeby Drive on right, with care turn left across road to climb stile and follow edge of field with fence on right. At woodland ahead, turn half left to continue along field edge to reach road after stile, here turn left along road and at end of woodland (Curr's Copse) on right, turn right into sunken grassy track - Newell's Lane.

Where track reaches open field ahead, bear right and shortly left, to ascend between banks. At top of climb, just after passing under telephone wire, bear left for about 100 yards to climb stile next to metal gate at near corner of woodland (Noke End) - here is the choice of route. For the shorter walk, bear slightly left along edge of wood with fence on left to reach stile on left, here turn sharp left through middle of field towards centre of copse in hollow on far boundary. Turn half left through the copse, pass over a pair of stiles and continue in same direction through middle of field to reach stile at track (Jackson's Lane), here turn left to rejoin the longer route.

For the longer walk, turn right along broad grass track, then after stile next to metal gate, pass between the buildings of Rose Farm and continue on concrete farm road curving right. At track junction, leave concrete road and keep straight on through field ahead towards middle of woodland. Enter woodland ahead (Park Wood) and, on emerging from mature trees with open views ahead, ignore track to right but turn left downhill on narrow winding path. Since the devastating storm of October 1987 the hillside has been completely replanted with oak, beech and ash. After passing monument on left follow steeply descending path to reach stile at bottom of hillside. Continue down middle of field, past 'lonesome pine' to meet concrete road after another stile, here turn left to continue the walk - or turn right to visit the picturesque Thameside village of Mapledurham (no direct access to river) with its flint and brick parish church of St. Margaret's. Mapledurham House and Mill (the oldest mill on the Thames) are open to the public at weekends during the summer.

Continue on concrete road, passing Park Farm on left. On reaching solitary bungalow, turn left up another concrete farm road, then at fork ahead, go right up further concrete road, past farm buildings on right, in direction of Chazey Wood. Continue on winding road through the wood to eventually reach junction of tracks by thatched cottage at end of concrete road, here turn left along fenced farm track, Jackson's Lane. At stile on left, the shorter walk enters from the left. At end of track, pass through gap next to metal gate, turn right along road for about 50 yards and with care cross main road (A4074) to return to the old road at start.

Footnote MAPLEDURHAM HOUSE: Open from Easter Sunday to end of September, Saturdays, Sundays & Public Holidays, 2.30-5.00. WATER MILL: 1.30-5.00.

DATE WALKED | | | 19 |

Ramble No. 8

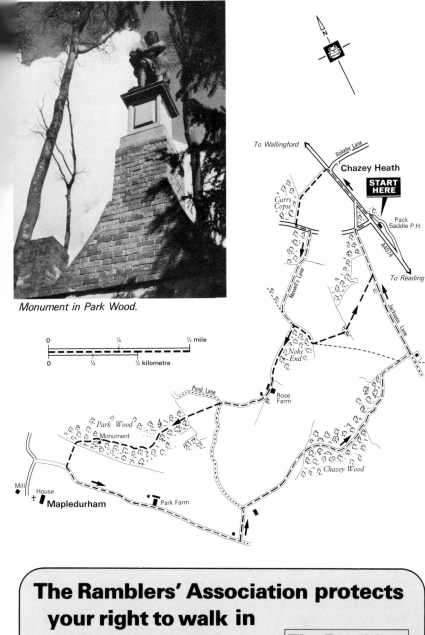

Monument in Park Wood.

To Wallingford

Rokeby Lane

Chazey Heath

START HERE

Currs Copse

Pack Saddle P.H.

A4074

To Reading

Newell's Lane

Jacksons Lane

Noke End

Rose Farm

Pond Lane

Park Wood

Monument

Chazey Wood

Mill

House

+ **Mapledurham**

Park Farm

0 ¼ ½ mile
0 ¼ ½ kilometre

Tinker's Green and Hemdean Bottom

distance 6 mile

This circular walk, of about 6 miles in length, on the very outskirts of Reading, is through pleasant undulating farmland and woodland.

The directions below start from the car park at Mapledurham playing fields (Grid Ref. 698758), but the map of the route may suggest other starting places or shorter alternatives. For further topographical features of the area, see the Ordnance Survey Pathfinder map 1172 'Reading'. Please observe the Country Code; in particular, keep to footpaths, keep dogs on lead across farmland and leave all wild flowers for others to enjoy.

From entrance to Mapledurham playing fields, turn left along Upper Woodcote Road (A4074) for just over 1/4 mile and between properties Nos. 185 & 187 turn left into gravel track. After stile ahead, just beyond 'Lane Cottage', go half-right along edge of field with fence on right to stile in far corner, here turn right along track (Jacksons Lane) for about 80 yards, then left for about 50 yards along concrete road. Now turn right over stile and bear half left through middle of field, passing power line pole on left, to another stile. Maintain same direction in next two fields, to cross small valley and to reach stile in middle of trees on far field boundary, here turn right to follow fence on right.

After stile at path junction, continue ahead on grassy track, then after about 100 yards where this track (Newell's Lane) bends right, keep straight on into field passing three large trees on right, to shortly enter corner of field ahead. Now go diagonally down through middle of field to far corner, in direction of distant pylon, just to left of white house. Now bear left along track and then concrete road through buildings of Pithouse Farm to road ahead, here continue ahead on grassy track across Trench Green and shortly keep straight on along road. When road bends left, keep straight on through gateway to brick cottages on left and pass through metal swing gate at far end of garden, here after about 40 yards ahead, turn

right over stile. Continue through middle of long field to metal field gate in far boundary, just to right of thatched 'Well Cottage' at Tinkers Green.

Cross over road (Sheepways Lane) to enter fenced track ahead and to pass buildings of Greendene Farm on left before reaching road (A4074), here with care cross over and turn left along verge. After about 80 yards, turn right into broad woodland path and near end of this wooded strip, go right to soon enter fenced path. Just beyond end of field on left, turn left along narrow path through trees. Shortly after two stiles close together in corner of field enter Bardolph's Wood and continue on waymarked (painted white arrows) woodland path to reach road (Tokersgreen Lane) after stile, here turn right along road for just over 1/4 mile. Where road bears right at property 'Scarletts', fork left and then turn sharp left, along tarmac road. At gateway to large property ahead, fork right into gently descending track.

In bottom of hollow, go over stile ahead and continue straight on steeply up through middle of field to another stile, here enter narrow hedged and fenced path to reach road ahead by a further stile. Now turn right along winding gravel track to eventually descend to road (Gravel Hill), here continue straight on between farm buildings on left and red brick Shipnell Cottages on right into fenced track and follow this along the length of Hemdean Bottom (known locally as 'Buggs Bottom').

At road ahead, turn right into Sheridan Avenue and at top of rise turn right into Wrenfield Drive, then between Nos. 45 and 18 enter fenced tarmac path to reach road. Now turn right along Kidmore Road for about 80 yards, then turn left and cross into Richmond Road, and at junction at far end, turn right along Woodcote Road (A4074) to return to playing fields on left at start.

Ramble No. 9

DATE WALKED | | 19

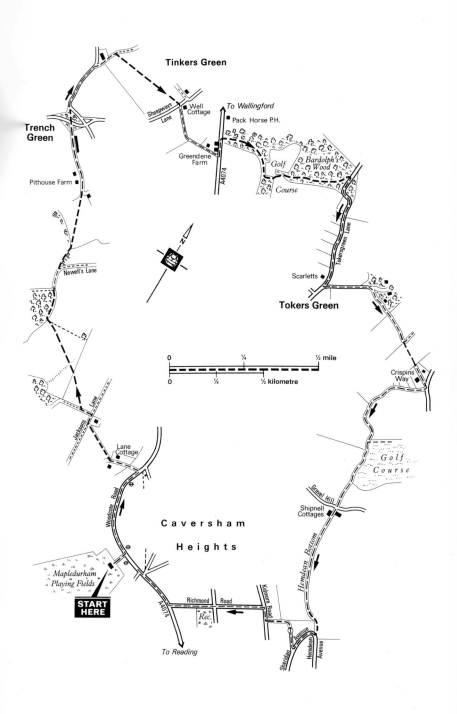

Tinkers Green

Sheepways Lane

Well Cottage

To Wallingford

Pack Horse P.H.

Trench Green

Greendene Farm

Pithouse Farm

A4074

Golf *Bardolph's Wood*

Course

Newell's Lane

Tokers-green Lane

Scarletts

Tokers Green

0   ¼   ½ mile

0   ¼   ½ kilometre

Crispins Way

Jacksons Lane

Lane Cottage

Golf
Course

Gravel Hill

Shipnell Cottages

Woodcote Road

C a v e r s h a m

H e i g h t s

Hemdean Bottom

Mapledurham Playing Fields

START HERE

A4074

Richmond   Road

Kidmore Road

Rec.

Sheridan Avenue

Hemdean Avenue

To Reading

Balmore Walk and Sonning Eye

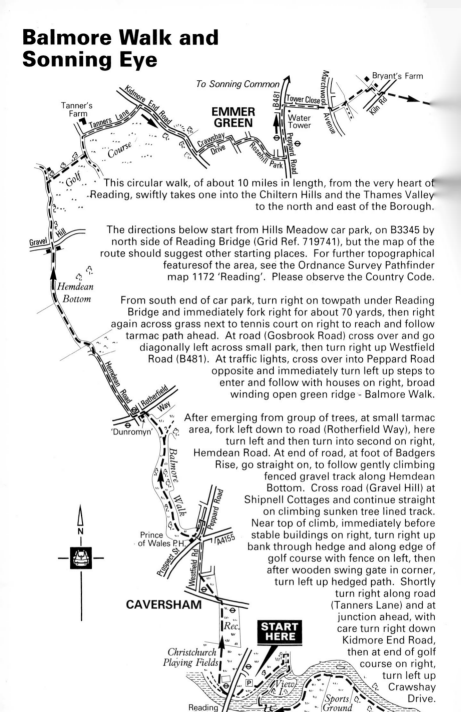

This circular walk, of about 10 miles in length, from the very heart of Reading, swiftly takes one into the Chiltern Hills and the Thames Valley to the north and east of the Borough.

The directions below start from Hills Meadow car park, on B3345 by north side of Reading Bridge (Grid Ref. 719741), but the map of the route should suggest other starting places. For further topographical features of the area, see the Ordnance Survey Pathfinder map 1172 'Reading'. Please observe the Country Code.

From south end of car park, turn right on towpath under Reading Bridge and immediately fork right for about 70 yards, then right again across grass next to tennis court on right to reach and follow tarmac path ahead. At road (Gosbrook Road) cross over and go diagonally left across small park, then turn right up Westfield Road (B481). At traffic lights, cross over into Peppard Road opposite and immediately turn left up steps to enter and follow with houses on right, broad winding open green ridge - Balmore Walk.

After emerging from group of trees, at small tarmac area, fork left down to road (Rotherfield Way), here turn left and then turn into second on right, Hemdean Road. At end of road, at foot of Badgers Rise, go straight on, to follow gently climbing fenced gravel track along Hemdean Bottom. Cross road (Gravel Hill) at Shipnell Cottages and continue straight on climbing sunken tree lined track. Near top of climb, immediately before stable buildings on right, turn right up bank through hedge and along edge of golf course with fence on left, then after wooden swing gate in corner, turn left up hedged path. Shortly turn right along road (Tanners Lane) and at junction ahead, with care turn right down Kidmore End Road, then at end of golf course on right, turn left up Crawshay Drive.

Ramble No. 10

distance 10 miles

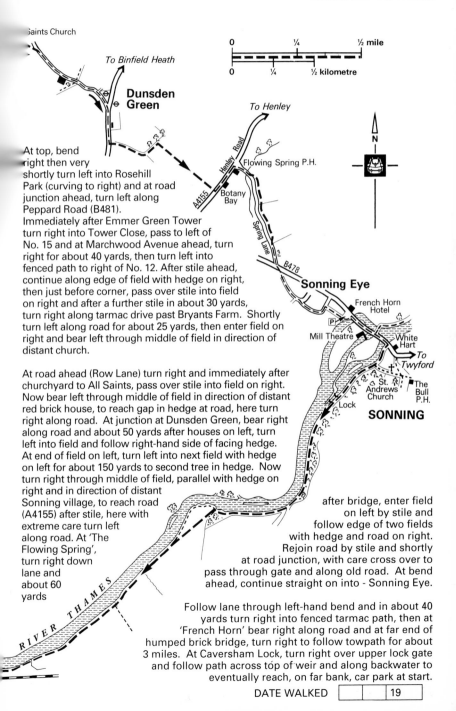

At top, bend right then very shortly turn left into Rosehill Park (curving to right) and at road junction ahead, turn left along Peppard Road (B481). Immediately after Emmer Green Tower turn right into Tower Close, pass to left of No. 15 and at Marchwood Avenue ahead, turn right for about 40 yards, then turn left into fenced path to right of No. 12. After stile ahead, continue along edge of field with hedge on right, then just before corner, pass over stile into field on right and after a further stile in about 30 yards, turn right along tarmac drive past Bryants Farm. Shortly turn left along road for about 25 yards, then enter field on right and bear left through middle of field in direction of distant church.

At road ahead (Row Lane) turn right and immediately after churchyard to All Saints, pass over stile into field on right. Now bear left through middle of field in direction of distant red brick house, to reach gap in hedge at road, here turn right along road. At junction at Dunsden Green, bear right along road and about 50 yards after houses on left, turn left into field and follow right-hand side of facing hedge. At end of field on left, turn left into next field with hedge on left for about 150 yards to second tree in hedge. Now turn right through middle of field, parallel with hedge on right and in direction of distant Sonning village, to reach road (A4155) after stile, here with extreme care turn left along road. At 'The Flowing Spring', turn right down lane and about 60 yards

after bridge, enter field on left by stile and follow edge of two fields with hedge and road on right. Rejoin road by stile and shortly at road junction, with care cross over to pass through gate and along old road. At bend ahead, continue straight on into - Sonning Eye.

Follow lane through left-hand bend and in about 40 yards turn right into fenced tarmac path, then at 'French Horn' bear right along road and at far end of humped brick bridge, turn right to follow towpath for about 3 miles. At Caversham Lock, turn right over upper lock gate and follow path across top of weir and along backwater to eventually reach, on far bank, car park at start.

DATE WALKED | | 19

Nunhide Lane and Horsemoor Wood

distance 3¼ or 5 mile

This circular walk, of about 5 miles in length, is through the beautiful rolling countryside immediately west of Reading, with extensive views over the hills surrounding the valley of the River Pang. Within the route is described a shorter alternative of 3¼ miles.

The directions below start from the Turnhams Farm recreation ground in Little Heath Road, Tilehurst (Grid. Ref. 654728), but the map of the route may suggest other starting places or alternative walks. For further topographical features of the area, see the Ordnance Survey Pathfinder map 1172 'Reading'. Please observe the Country Code.

With your back to recreation ground, turn right along road and immediately after house on right, turn right over stile to follow edge of two fields with fence and then hedge on right. Enter woods (Harefield Copse) ahead by stile and descend on well defined woodland path, then emerge to cross over end of field by two more stiles. Continue straight on through middle of very large field passing, away to the right, a red brick tower, the remains of a dovecot, then at end of field turn right along gravel farm road - Nunhide Lane.

Pass the buildings of Nunhide Farm on right and immediately after pair of red brick cottages on left, fork left to follow edge of large field with hedge on left. At end of field is your choice of route. For the shorter walk of 3¼ miles, keep straight on along edge of field ahead with hedge and then Horsemoor Wood on left to stile at far end, here turn right to join the longer route again. For the longer walk, turn left through middle of field, keeping parallel to, but away from, hedge on left, in direction of M4 motorway. After footbridge over stream, bear slightly left shortly to cross M4 by footbridge with spiral approaches.

Continue straight on with fence and large buildings of Malpas Farm on right, then after stile next to metal gate at Pond Farm, follow tarmac road through right and left-hand bends. When road bends left again, just after overhead power lines, turn right along winding hedged track eventually to reach edge of M4, here turn left over stile into fenced path with road on right. After stile ahead, cross M4 by road bridge keeping to verge on right, then shortly after end of crash barrier on right, turn sharp right into tarmac track soon to reach Hogmoor Bridge over the River Pang.

Continue on hedged gravel track through left and right-hand bends and at start of second field on left, turn left over stile next to metal gate to follow edge of field with hedge on left. Shortly at copse on left, bear slightly right through middle of field to enter field ahead by stile and to follow edge of field with hedge on left. Enter wood (Horsemoor Wood) ahead by stile and after emerging by footbridge, go ahead for about 50 yards to rejoin the shorter walk at stile on right. Keep along edge of field with fence still on right and after stile in far corner, turn left through middle of long narrow field towards buildings of Sulham Farm and just before end of field, turn right over stile and up short track to farm road ahead (Nunhide Lane). To continue walk turn right, but turn left for about 80 yards to visit the small but impressive church of St. Nicholas, Sulham. Built in 1832, it replaced one that had stood on or near this site since the late 13th century.

After passing through gateway, keep along farm road, then where this bends left, turn left through small metal swing gate and continue on well-defined path through middle of field to stile into woods on far boundary. In about 10 yards, turn left to follow climbing woodland path shortly to enter field again by another stile, here continue along field edge to enter woods again by a further stile. Continue steeply up grass path and in top corner to right, after stile enter hedged track (Kiln Lane) to reach road ahead, here cross over and turn right along footway of Little Heath Road for about ½ mile to return to recreation ground at start.

Ramble No. 11

DATE WALKED | | 19

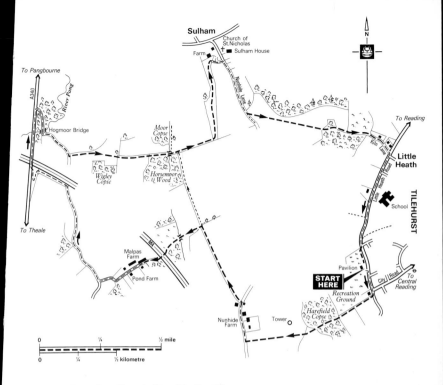

The path to Dunsden Church. (Ramble No. 10)

River Kennet and Sulhamstead Bannister

distance 6³/₄ miles

This circular walk, of about 6³/₄ miles in length, to the south of Theale, provides a marked contrast in scenery, from the waterways and lakes of the Lower Kennet Water Park to the undulating farmland and meadows around Sulhamstead. For ease of access, this walk takes advantage of a new public footpath between Wigmore Lane and the River Kennet.

The directions below start from near the south end of Wigmore Lane, Theale (Grid Ref. 633703) where there is room for parking on verge, but the map of the route may suggest other starting places or shorter alternatives. For further topographical features of the area, see the Ordnance Survey Pathfinder maps 1172 'Reading' and 1188 'Mortimer and Arborfield'. Please observe the Country Code; in particular, keep to footpaths, keep dogs on lead across farmland and leave all wild flowers for others to enjoy.

Continue to the south end of Wigmore Lane, with care cross railway line by stiles and turn right along fenced gravel path. At first power line pole ahead turn left, then after passing through copse, cross wooden footbridge and turn right along the winding north bank of River Kennet. On reaching footbridge and weir, turn left across bridge to now follow bank of Kennet and Avon Canal. At Sulhamstead Swing Bridge ahead, turn right over bridge and then turn left along towpath for just over ¹/₂ mile. Immediately after crossing concrete footbridge, turn sharp right along woodland strip with river on right and lake on left. At end of first lake on left, ignore path turning left and continue ahead past second lake to reach road.

At road junction, continue ahead along road, then immediately after property 'The Oaks', turn left up tarmac road and at entrance to Highways Training Centre continue on grassy track curving right. At end of Brick Kiln Copse on left, pass through metal gate and bear left through middle of field (passing to right of pylon), to reach stile to right of large red brick house (The Old Manor), here

turn right along gravel track passing white 'Thane Cottage' on right. At road ahead, turn right down road and immediately next to white 'Keepers Cottage' on left, fork left up private tarmac road. On reaching concrete surface (before Home Farm) fork left into climbing fenced grass track. Enter field ahead and continue along edge with fence on right to stile in far corner, here turn half right to follow fence on left and shortly after further stile, enter St Michael's Burial Ground at Sulhamstead Bannister Upper End. All that now remains of the flint-faced St Michael's Church, built in 1912, is the porch - left as a shelter for funeral mourners.

At road ahead, turn right past 'The Old School' and at bend in road, keep straight on over stile and immediately turn left, down edge of field with fence on left to reach another stile at road, here with care turn right down road (Kingston Lane). At end of second field on right, fork right to follow descending edge of field with hedge on right. At end of field, pass through small wooden swing gate and immediately turn right for about 20 yards to pass over footbridge and stile into field. Now turn left to follow edge of field along two sides with fence on left. At stile in second corner, turn left steeply downhill through woodland with fence on right, to reach road junction, here turn right along road (Bottom Lane) passing 'Glen Lodge' on right.

Immediately before the white 'Hazel Cottage' on left, turn left over stile and down edge of field shortly to cross large wooden footbridge with integral stiles - built by Reading Ramblers in 1977 (see plaque midway along handrail). After stile adjacent to bridge, continue straight on through water meadow following ditch on left, to reach after metal field gate, Sulhamstead Swing Bridge again. Now cross bridge and turn left to retrace route used at beginning of walk, to return to the start.

DATE WALKED | | | 19 |

Ramble No. 12

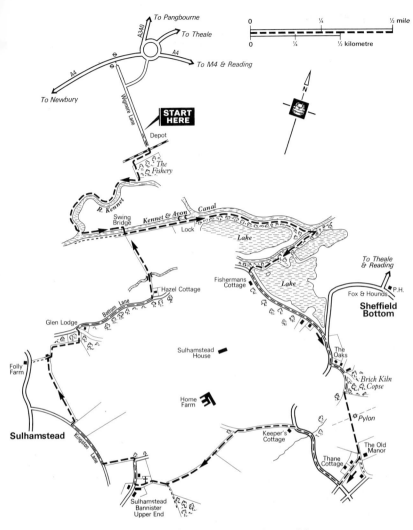

To Pangbourne

A340

To Theale

A4

To M4 & Reading

A4

To Newbury

0   ¼   ½ mile
0   ¼   ½ kilometre

N

Wigmore Lane

START HERE

Depot

The Fishery

R. Kennet

Swing Bridge

Kennet & Avon Canal

Lock

Lake

To Theale & Reading

Fishermans Cottage

Lake

Fox & Hounds P.H.

Sheffield Bottom

Hazel Cottage

Bottom Lane

Glen Lodge

Sulhamstead House

The Oaks

Brick Kiln Copse

Folly Farm

Home Farm

Pylon

Sulhamstead

Kingston Lane

Keeper's Cottage

The Old Manor

Thane Cottage

Sulhamstead Bannister Upper End

The longest footbridge to be built in Berkshire using voluntary labour.

Ufton Nervet and Shootersbrook Lane   distance 4 1/2 miles

This circular walk, of about 4 1/2 miles in length, through undulating farmland to the west of Burghfield, provides extensive views across and along the Kennet Valley.

The directions below start from the south side of St. Peter's Church, Ufton Nervet (Grid Ref. 635675), but the map of the route may suggest other starting places or shorter alternatives. For further topographical features of the area, see the Ordnance Survey Pathfinder map 1188 'Mortimer and Arborfield'. Please observe the Country Code; in particular, keep to footpaths, keep dogs on lead across farmland and leave all wild flowers for others to enjoy.

With the Church of St. Peter (built in 1861) on your right, go ahead to road junction and turn left along Camp Road for about 50 yards to turn right along fenced, gravel and then grass track. After pink washed Ufton Court Lodge on left, cross road and continue straight on along tarmac drive between broad avenue of oaks towards the Elizabethan front of Ufton Court. The house, which dates from the late 15th century, was the home of the Perkins family, Catholic recusants who gave sanctuary to many priests in the days of Elizabeth 1. At crossing track before house, turn right along track for about 60 yards to just before old oak, then fork left into descending track - Shootersbrook Lane.

Cross bridge over Brent's Gully and at top of long climb ahead, pass through metal farm gate, then after about 30 yards turn right between buildings of Old Farm. Leaving farm yard, enter broad track and after 60 yards turn half right over stile. Go diagonally down through middle of large field to reach stile at left-hand end of Noormoor Copse on right. Follow edge of copse, on right, to cross stream and continue in field ahead with hedge on right. In next field keep along field-edge track with Ashen Wood on right, and after stile next to wooden gate, continue on fenced track to reach road opposite Middle Farm, here turn left down road keeping to verge on right.

On approaching road junction, fork right across grass to turn right up Church Lane passing remains of chapel on left and 'Dog and Partridge' (once a public house) on right. Immediately before Uftongreen Farm, turn left over stile and pass farm buildings. Shortly on right, look to horizon for spire of church at Ufton Nervet.

At end of field on left follow track over stream and bear slightly right through middle of field to small footbridge. Continue along edge of next field with fence and trees on left to reach road by houses at Sulhamstead.

Now turn left along road and shortly at junction, turn right with care up road (Kingston Lane), then near top of climb, turn left over stile along edge of field with fence on right. By first oak tree at top of rise, turn right over stile next to metal gate and continue along road to Sulhamstead Bannister Upper End, passing 'The Old School' and St. Michael's Burial Ground on left, and Meales Farm on right. All that now remains of the flint-faced St. Michael's Church, built in 1912, is the porch - left as a shelter for funeral mourners. At road junction ahead, enter fenced gravel track opposite, cross over at next road ahead (Sulhamstead Road) and after stile in hedge, follow edge of field with row of trees on right. Then bear right over stile into next field and continue along edge with fence on left to reach road (Church Lane) after stile, here turn left along road to return to the church at start.

DATE WALKED   19

Ramble No. 13

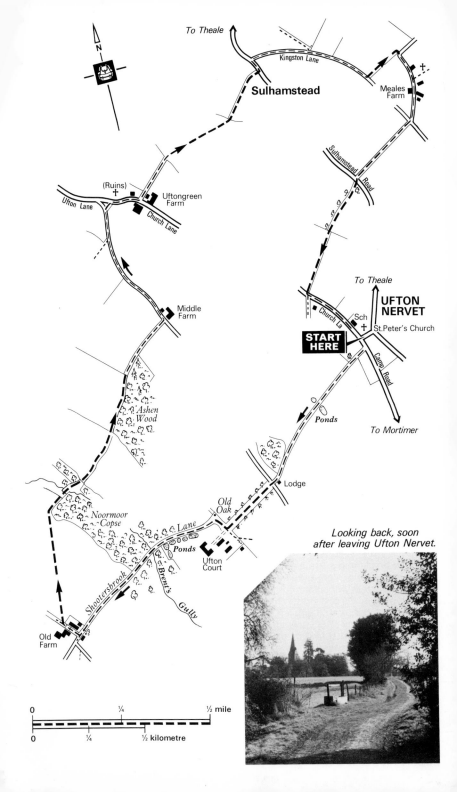

To Theale

Kingston Lane

Sulhamstead

Meales Farm

✝

Ufton Lane

(Ruins) ✝

Uftongreen Farm

Church Lane

Sulhamstead Road

Middle Farm

To Theale

UFTON NERVET

Church La

Sch

✝ St. Peter's Church

START HERE

Camp. Road

To Mortimer

Ashen Wood

Ponds

Lodge

Noormoor Copse

Old Oak

Lane

Ponds

Shootersbrook

Brent's Gully

Ufton Court

Old Farm

0		¼		½ mile

0		¼		½ kilometre

Looking back, soon after leaving Ufton Nervet.

Pullen's Pond and Starvale Woods

distance 4 miles

This circular walk, of about 4 miles in length, north of Mortimer, has an attractive mixture of heathland, woodland and farmland, with some surprisingly pleasant open views to the east.

The directions below start from Burghfield Village Hall car park (entry from Recreation Road), Grid Ref. 652667, but the map of the route may suggest other starting places or shorter alternatives. For further topographical features of the area, see the Ordnance Survey Pathfinder map 1188 'Mortimer and Arborfield'. Please observe the Country Code; in particular, keep to footpaths, keep dogs on lead across farmland and leave all wild flowers for others to enjoy.

From car park, turn left along main road (Reading Road) and immediately after garage, take lower path on left through woodland keeping parallel to road. Just before houses ahead, turn right across road between shops in Bunces Lane and a few yards after passing through right-hand bend, turn left into fenced and hedged tarmac path. On joining gravel track (Spring Wood Lane) follow this through left-hand bend and at end, before property 'Reids', turn right down concrete steps into hedged path to enter, after small stream, woodland ahead. At top of short climb, fork left on well defined path and at crossing gravel track, turn left along this track. At red brick cottage ahead continue on track to right, shortly to pass on right at bottom of descent - Pullen's Pond.

Continue on climbing winding track to road (Goring Lane), here turn left along road for about 30 yards, then turn sharp right along gravel track shortly to turn left down another road (Lockram Road). Just over 100 yards after Lockram Farmhouse on right, turn right through gap in fence. Pass to right of two mid-field trees before crossing wooden foot-bridge spanning Lockram Brook. Continue ahead in next field and at left-hand bend bear left through gap in fence, passing small pond on right to soon reach stile at top of climb. Here turn right along edge of field with fence on right, and at field boundary on left, turn left down edge of field with fence on right. At end of field, turn right over stile to follow edge of two sides of next field, with fence and then trees on left. Just before buildings of Mann's Farm near top of climb, turn left through gap in fence, down steps and over two foot-bridges to reach road through another gap in fence, here turn right along road, (Nightingale Lane).

Just after kink in road, turn left along side of field, with wooden fence on right. Just before end of this field, pass through metal swing gate ahead, and bear right through middle of next field (under power lines) to large oak tree on far boundary. Enter woodland ahead through gap in fence and keep right until reaching road (Hammond's Heath). Now keep straight on along edge of 'The Fairground', parallel with road (Windmill Road) on right, entering and leaving by metal swing gates. On rejoining road and shortly reaching conifer woodland on right, turn right to follow wire mesh fence on right. At end of fence, keep straight on through woodland (Windmill Common) with field shortly nearby on left. After crossing small valley with stream in bottom, pass to the left of the red brick Bridges Farm and turn right along road (Longmoor Lane), then where road bends right, turn left into broad path through woodland - Starvale Woods.

Follow path slowly curving left, then at path junction in slight hollow, turn right down path between conifer plantations. Cross over Lockram Brook again and climb up to pass through wooden swing gates at both ends of fenced path next to red brick cottage (Starvale Cottage) on left. Continue ahead on woodland path across Wokefield Common to reach near side of pond, here turn right to soon reach and cross road junction.

Follow left-hand of two paths through woodland ahead (way-marked with painted white arrows), and immediately

continued on next page

Ramble No. 14

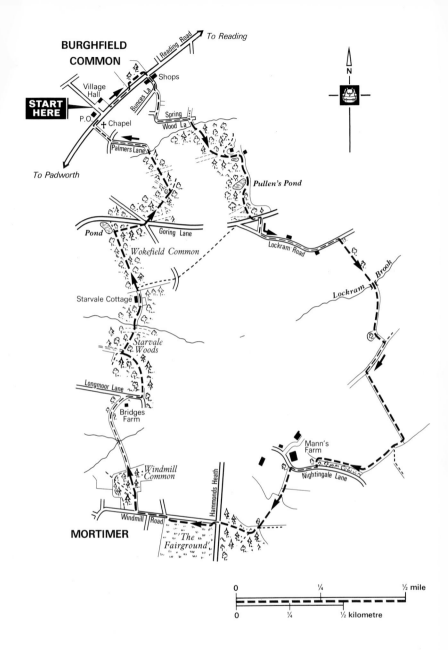

after small pond on left turn left. Cross over gravel track and shortly pass over tiny stream to enter hedged surfaced path before houses ahead. Now turn left along gravel road (Palmers Lane), cross over road ahead into hedged and fenced path, and at end by Methodist Church, turn right along road to return to Burghfield Common and the car park at start.

DATE WALKED   19

Admiral's Copse and Foudry Brook

distance 4½ miles

This circular walk, of about 4½ miles in length, from Stratfield Mortimer, is through the very pleasant and gently undulating rural landscape on the Berkshire/Hampshire border.

The directions below start from Mortimer Station (Grid Ref. 672641), but the map of the route may suggest other starting places. For further topographical features of the area, see the Ordnance Survey Pathfinder map 1188 'Mortimer and Arborfield'. Please observe the Country Code; in particular, keep to footpaths, keep dogs on lead across farmland and leave all wild flowers for others to enjoy.

Leaving railway station by access road, turn left along road (Station Road) and immediately after crossing bridge (Tun Bridge) over stream (Foudry Brook), turn right along road, then after last house on left, turn left into climbing fenced path between fields. Cross over road (Mortimer Lane) to enter field opposite by squeeze stile, then keep straight on to follow wide grass strip to right of woodland. Continue ahead along fenced path, soon joining track from right, leading to Wheat's Farm at top of climb. Here keep straight on between farm buildings.

Cross over farm track ahead and immediately turn left up bank. After about 50 yards cross stile ahead to enter narrow path with ditch close on left. At path junction turn left over stile into field on left and after about 20 yards turn right along edge of this field with hedge on right. Ignore small wooden gate on right, and after about 20 yards, enter field ahead by stile and continue down edge of field with hedge on right. After next stile continue along gravel track and at road (The Street) ahead, cross over and turn right along footway, then near top of rise turn left into soon descending gravel track, Kiln Lane. At bottom of descent, follow narrow path along wooden fence to left of 'Ashfield'. Cross footbridge over stream and in about 10 yards, turn left over stile into fenced path with ditch on left, shortly to enter woodland ahead - Admiral's Copse.

Follow well-defined path through length of woodland and at far end keep straight on through middle of field to red brick house at road (Drury Lane) ahead, here turn left down road. At junction, turn right down road (Pitfield Lane), then immediately before bridge (Tanhouse Bridge) over Foudry Brook, turn left into short hedged path and after stile, follow edge of field with stream on right. In corner of field go STRAIGHT AHEAD over two stiles, with stream between. With hedge on right shortly cross metal bridge over railway. Keep right along edge of field with fence on right to reach road after stile. Here turn left along road - the Berks/Hants County boundary and the Devil's Highway (the Roman road from London to Silchester).

Just past near corner of copse on right, turn left over stile next to metal farm gate to follow edge of two fields with fence on right - at beginning observe on right the remains of the once Ticklecorner Lane. Before end of second field, pass over stile next to metal farm gate to continue along broad grass track, with hedge now on left. After further stile ahead turn sharp left along hedged track below overhead power lines to another metal farm gate at end of track. Now follow hedge on right, then go ahead through middle of field, to reach and pass through metal gate and tunnel under railway. In next field, turn half right through middle of field to far corner, to reach wooden footbride over - Foudry Brook.

Do not cross bridge, but turn right over stile into fenced strip alongside brook on left. In field ahead follow hedge around property (Ladyfield House) on left, then, turn left up gravel track past the impressive tall stone church of St. Mary's to road ahead, here turn right along footway and then right over Tun Bridge again, to return to the station at the start.

DATE WALKED   [| | 19]

Ramble No. 15

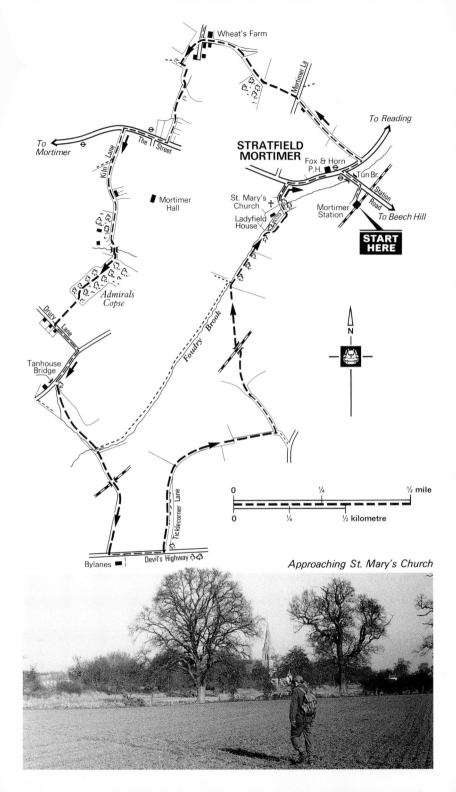

Wheat's Farm

Mortimer La

To Reading

STRATFIELD MORTIMER

To Mortimer

Kiln Lane

The Street

Fox & Horn P.H.

Tun Br.

Station Road

St. Mary's Church

Mortimer Hall

Ladyfield House

Mortimer Station

To Beech Hill

START HERE

N

Admirals Copse

Drury Lane

Foundry Brook

Tanhouse Bridge

0   ¼   ½ mile

0   ¼   ½ kilometre

Ticklecorner Lane

Bylanes

Devil's Highway

Approaching St. Mary's Church

Lambwoodhill Common and Brook Farm

distance 3½ miles

This circular walk, of nearly 3½ miles in length, from Grazeley, is entirely on paths and across the farmland on the western edge of the parish of Shinfield.

The directions below start from the church at Grazeley (Grid Ref. 699669), where there is limited parking on verge on south side of lane, but the map of the route may suggest other starting places. For further topographical features of the area, see the Ordnance Survey Pathfinder map 1188 'Mortimer and Arborfield'. Please observe the Country Code; in particular, keep to footpaths, keep dogs on lead across farmland and leave all wild flowers for others to enjoy.

With your back to the white swing gate of the small flint-faced Holy Trinity Church, go ahead along edge of recreation ground with fence on right. At far end, turn right through metal barrier and in about five yards pass through metal swing gate on right, then turn half left through middle of small field (football pitch) - part of Lambwoodhill Common.

After stiles ahead, maintain same direction in next field, to meet field boundary (approaching from right) at prominent waymarked post, here turn half left diagonally through middle of field in direction of most obvious pylon, to reach road (Pump Lane) after stile. Cross road to enter hedged track (Shepherdton Lane) opposite, pass under railway (Reading-Basingstoke line) and at end of grass lane, turn left along another grass track with ditch and long field on left. For the next 1½ miles the route will follow the Shinfield Parish boundary.

At end of field, turn left over wooden bridge and along another hedged track with ditch on right. With care pass through metal swing gates either side of railway and continue on track, then tarmac drive, with the buildings of Thurley Farm to the left. With care cross Bloomfield Hatch Lane ahead and after stile, keep along edge of large field with hedge on right to reach road after crossing ditch and stile. Now go slightly right to enter, through gateway opposite, fenced tarmac drive leading to Brook Farm - along here look left for distant views of Reading.

Continue ahead between farm buildings, then after gentle descent down tarmac drive, cross large new metal bridge (Reid's Bridge) over Foudry Brook and in about 50 yards, turn left into hedged track - Woodcock Lane. After about 200 yards, at end of copse on right, follow Foudry Brook on left, then where brook bends left, bear right up slope to follow fenced firm track with Swallowfield bypass on right.

Cross over road ahead past cattle grid and continue along fenced track with bypass above on right, to eventually pass through metal gate on left at the end. With your back to this gate, go half right though middle of field in a direction just to left of distant solitary white building ('The Wheatsheaf') to reach through gateway, wooden bridge over Foudry Brook. Now continue straight along field track with fence on left and ditch on right to reach road ahead by school, here cross over and keep along edge of recreation ground opposite, to return to the church at start.

DATE WALKED [ ][ ][19]

Ramble No. 16

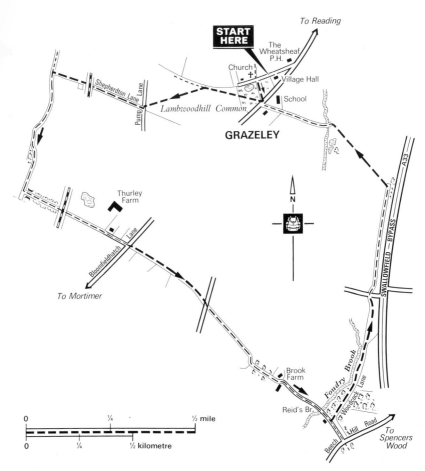

START HERE

To Reading

The Wheatsheaf P.H.

Church

Village Hall

School

Shepherdton Lane

Pump Lane

Lambwoodhill Common

GRAZELEY

Thurley Farm

Bloomfieldhatch Lane

To Mortimer

Brook Farm

Reid's Br.

Foudry Brook

SWALLOWFIELD – BYPASS

A33

Windock Lane

Beech Hill Road

To Spencers Wood

N

0	¼	½ mile
0	¼	½ kilometre

A windy day on Lambwoodhill Common.

Woodcock Lane and Three Mile Cross

distance 3½ miles

This mainly flat circular walk, of about 3½ miles in length, immediately to the south of Reading, is through the pastures and arable land that surrounds the village of Spencers Wood, part of Shinfield Parish. In winter and after wet weather, the early part of this walk can be rather muddy, so do go suitably shod.

The directions below start from the north end of the cul-de-sac in the old A33, left after the completion in 1980 of the new Swallowfield Bypass (Grid Ref. 715683), but the map of the route may suggest other starting places. For further topographical features of the area, see the Ordnance Survey Pathfinder map 1188 'Mortimer and Arborfield'. Please observe the Country Code; in particular, keep to footpaths, keep dogs on lead across farmland and leave all wild flowers for others to enjoy.

With your back to M4 motorway, go ahead along road and in front of first house on left 'Milestone Cottage', note old milestone 'Southampton 43' etc. At junction ahead (at 'Three Mile Cross' sign), with care cross road and turn right along footway for about 70 yards, then turn left through large metal gate into grass path - Woodcock Lane.

Follow this path for nearly 1½ miles, keeping Swallowfield Bypass nearby on right - the point at which you turn off the path is about 300 yards after following bypass close on right. Here turn left up track (Kiln Lane) through woodland strip keeping fields nearby on left, and at top of climb, just after woodland pond and stile on right, enter second field on left over stile and continue along edge of field with fence on left. Just after pond on left, pass through wooden swing gate to reach road (B3349), here with care cross road and turn left along footway into the centre of Spencers Wood village (population 4,000). Spencers Wood was originally one of the seven 'Hundreds' of Windsor Forest, but most of the development in its four main settlements did not take place until the end of the last century.

Just after United Reformed Church (and another milestone) turn right along Hyde End Road (B3349), then just past where road bends right, turn left along the length of Appletree Lane. At road junction ahead, turn right along road (Clares Green Road). At road junction, at end of field on left, fork left and in about 15 yards turn left along gravel track. Just before red brick pavilion on edge of playing fields, bear left into hedged path and after about 75 yards, bear right over stile into narrower path with fence on left and hedge on right.

After stile ahead, continue with hedge on right and now bushes on left, to a further stile. Keep along edge of next two fields, noting through gateway on right, view of Shire Hall on hilltop of Shinfield Park. Halfway along side of second field, cross stile and continue in same direction, with hedge now on left. After stile in corner of field enter hedged path shortly to reach road.

With care cross road and turn right, then shortly at the small Weslyan Chapel 1876 (Three Mile Cross Methodist Church) turn left into Grazely Road. Just after first pair of houses on right, turn right along tarmac path. Enter field ahead through bushes and follow right-hand edge to pass through gap in hedge in far corner, to rejoin Woodcock Lane again. Now turn right along this grass path and over road ahead, to return to parking place at start.

DATE WALKED [   ][   ][19]

Ramble No. 17

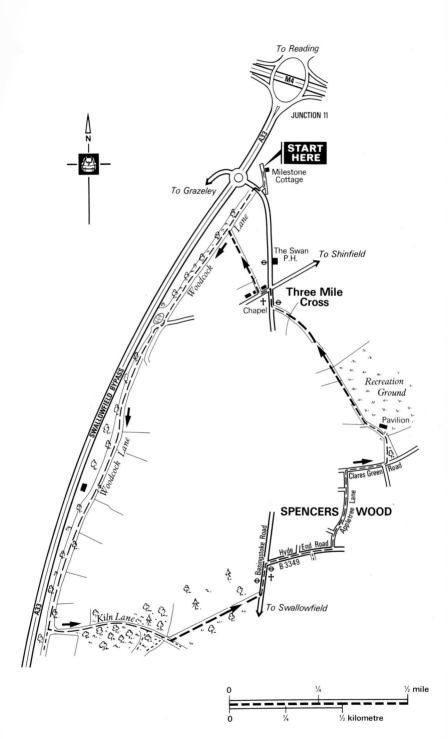

To Reading

M4

JUNCTION 11

A33

START HERE

Milestone Cottage

To Grazeley

Woodcock Lane

The Swan P.H.

To Shinfield

Three Mile Cross

Chapel

Swallowfield Bypass

Woodcock Lane

Recreation Ground

Pavilion

Clares Green Road

SPENCERS WOOD

Appletree Lane

Basingstoke Road

Hyde End Road

B 3349

A33

Kiln Lane

To Swallowfield

N

| 0 | ¼ | ½ mile |

| 0 | ¼ | ½ kilometre |

Shinfield Grange and Milkingbarn Lane

distance 4 miles

This circular walk, of about 4 miles in length, to the west of Arborfield, is over the rich agricultural land on both banks of the River Loddon.

The directions below start from the closed end of Cutbush Lane, Shinfield (Grid Ref. 741690) just north of Shinfield Grange, where there is ample room for roadside parking, but the map of the route may suggest other starting places. For further topographical features of the area, see the Ordnance Survey Pathfinder map 1188 'Mortimer and Arborfield'. Please observe the Country Code; in particular, keep to footpaths, keep dogs on lead across farmland and leave all wild flowers for others to enjoy.

With your back to M4 motorway, go ahead along Cutbush Lane and shortly after entrance to Shinfield Grange, turn left along tarmac road and at end of evergreen hedge on right, turn right into hedged grass track. After stile next to metal gate ahead, bear right along edge of long field with hedge on right and at end of field cross stile, then immediately turn sharp left diagonally through middle of field to stiles either side of short wooden footbridge. In next field, turn half right through middle of field to swing gate. Then maintain same

direction shortly to enter, after another stile, narrow path along edge of property 'The Magpie and Parrot' - once a public house.

After stile-way ahead, with care cross road and turn left along verge of main road (Arborfield Road, A327) to bridge over River Loddon. After a further 70 yards along road, immediately before the half timbered 'Bridge House', turn right into fenced path and after stile ahead, turn left along edge of field with fence on left. At corner of fence on left, turn right through middle of field to power line pole (keeping parallel with fence on left) to reach, after stile by pair of isolated trees, a farm track - Milkingbarn Lane. This lane was once a public bridlepath, to which the Parish Council agreed extinguishment in 1978, in exchange for Pound Copse, passed through later on this walk.

When over stile opposite, continue along edge of field with hedge on left and at end of second field on left, turn left over stile and along edge of field with fence on right. After further stile ahead, turn left on permitted path through Pound Copse with road nearby on right. At end of copse, rejoin public footpath entering from field edge on left,

Ramble No. 18

Sunshine in Shinfield

hen pass through stileway on right and
urn left along road, Greensward Lane.
At road junction ahead, turn right along
main road (A327) for about 100 yds, then
cross over into Church Lane and when
this road bends right, turn left into
tarmac 'No Through Road'.

After right-hand bend in road, by 'The
Old Rectory' on right, enter land of NIRD
(National Institute for Research into
Dairying) by white swing gate next to

cattle grid. Continue ahead along
tree-lined avenue and immediately after
crossing junction with concrete road,
look left for the remains of the earlier
Arborfield Church. Keep to tarmac road
and shortly enter gravel track with
Youngstock Unit of Hall Farm on right,
then after stile next to metal gate, follow
field edge to soon cross bridge over
River Loddon and a further stile next to
metal gate.

Continue straight on along edge of next
field with fence on left and after stile
next to metal gate, enter broad hedged
track. After about 350 yards, when near
to far end of the distant buildings of
Oldhouse Farm on right, turn right over
stile into hedged and fenced path, and
after stile and footbridge at far side of
field ahead, enter fenced path with ditch
on left. After railway sleeper footbridge,
continue along fenced path through next
field to reach stile at road and turn left to
return to parking place at start.

DATE WALKED | | | 19 |

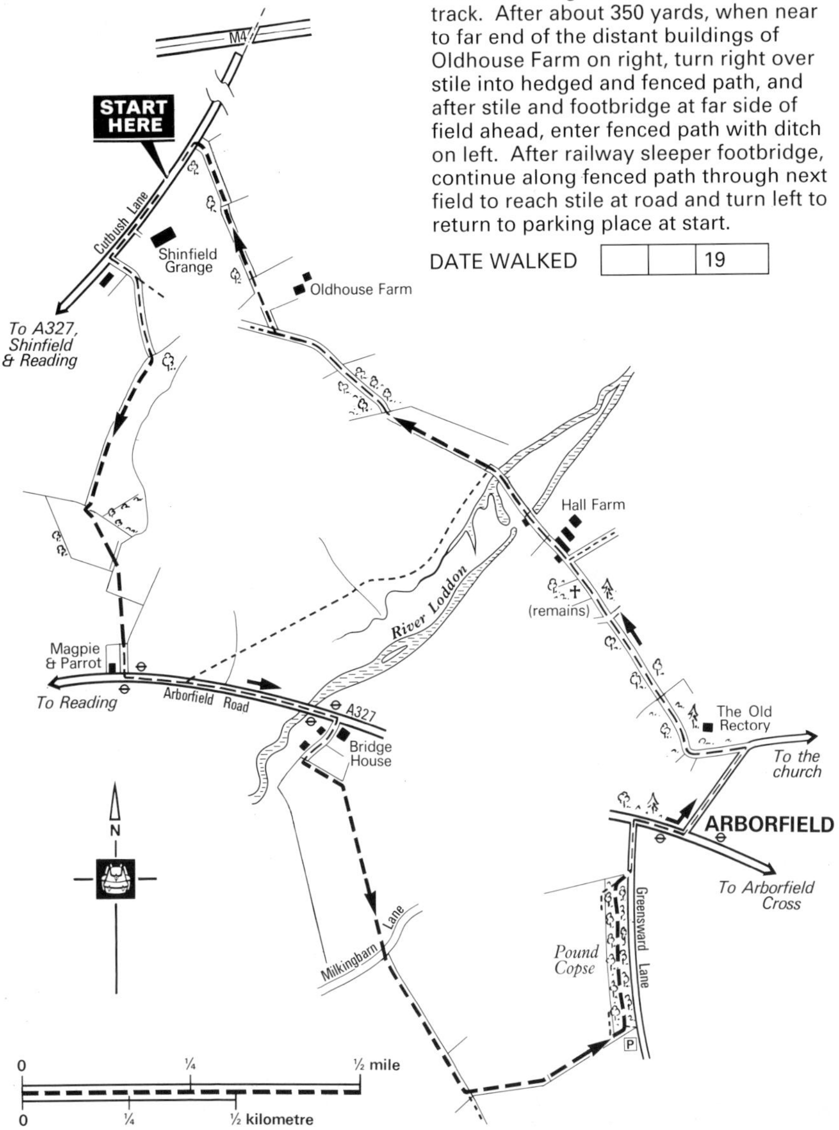

START HERE

Cutbush Lane

M4

Shinfield Grange

Oldhouse Farm

To A327,
Shinfield
& Reading

Hall Farm

+ (remains)

River Loddon

The Old
Rectory

To the
church

Magpie
& Parrot

To Reading   Arborfield Road

A327

Bridge
House

ARBORFIELD

To Arborfield
Cross

N

Pound
Copse

Greensward Lane

Milkingbarn Lane

P

0   ¼   ½ mile

0   ¼   ½ kilometre

Carter's Hill and Barkham Brook

distance 4½ miles

This circular walk, of about 4½ miles in length, includes both the flat rich agricultural land and the gently undulating woodland to the north of Arborfield Cross. In winter and after wet weather, some of the paths can be rather muddy, so do go suitably shod.

The directions below start from the small free car park at Arborfield Cross (Grid Ref. 760670) which is situated about 200 yards down the Swallowfield Road from 'The Bull'. For further topographical features of the area see the Ordnance Survey Pathfinder map 1188 'Mortimer and Arborfield'. Please observe the Country Code; in particular, keep to footpaths, keep dogs on lead across farmland and leave all wild flowers for others to enjoy.

Leaving car park, turn left up road and at 'The Bull' with great care cross main road (A327) into Sindlesham Road (B3030) opposite, passing between 'Best Kept Village' plaques on left and War Memorial on right. Continue along road for about ¼ mile keeping to verge on right, then just before right-hand bend, with care turn left across road and over stile into field. Keep along edge of field with hedge on left, then immediately after tall overhead power lines, fork left over stile into fenced and hedged path to reach gravel track at entrance to Cloud Stables and metalled road ahead. If you wish to visit the impressive flint-faced Arborfield Parish Church of St. Bartholomew, built in 1863, turn left along road for about 60 yards.

To continue walk turn right along road. Immediately after 'The Old Reading Room' (1881) on left, turn sharp left into winding gravel track (Cartershill Lane) to pass Monks Cottage and eventually reach gate with large farm buildings away to the left - here ignore concrete road and turn right through another metal gate along farm track (Barretts Lane). At overhead power lines keep right, down winding gravel track to pass over Barkham Brook, by footbridge next to ford, below Carter's Hill Farm.

At top of short sharp rise ahead, turn right along road for about 40 yards, then fork right along wide farm track (Copse Barnhill Lane) and at road ahead (B3030), with care cross over to enter gently climbing tree-lined track (Gravelpithill Lane). After slight right bend just before top of hill, turn left at ladder stile to shortly emerge from woodland by a similar stile. Cross further stile 15 yards ahead and then bear right through middle of two fields to reach double stile where field boundary meets woodland on right - from this path look left for the red brick Bearwood College, the Royal Merchant Navy School, overlooking the large, unseen Bear Wood Lake .

From stile go half-right for 75 yards across narrow woodland strip to reach swing gate. Here turn left along sandy track (Coombes Lane) for about 20 yards and turn right through stileway into path through rhododendrons. Shortly pass metal gate and follow path through right-hand bend and continue gently downhill to eventually reach junction of paths adjacent to near corner of field on right, here continue straight on with field nearby on right. At end of this field, turn sharp right into tree-lined path (Wood Lane) and at top of climb turn left along slowly descending track (Cole Lane). After crossing Barkham Brook again, by concrete footbridge next to ford, continue on track ahead to eventually reach Arborfield Cross again, here with care cross over road junction into Swallowfield Road to return to car park at start.

DATEWALKED   19

Ramble No. 19

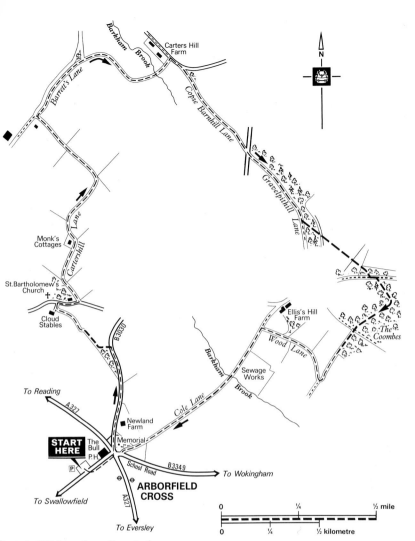

To Reading
A327

START HERE The Bull P.H.

ARBORFIELD CROSS

To Swallowfield

To Eversley
A327

School Road
B3349
To Wokingham

Memorial

Newland Farm

Cole Lane

Barkham Brook

Sewage Works

Wood Lane

Ellis's Hill Farm

The Coombes

Barkham Brook

B3030

Cloud Stables

St. Bartholomew's Church

Monk's Cottages

Cartershill Lane

Barrett's Lane

Carters Hill Farm

Barkham Brook

Copse Barnhill Lane

Gravelpithill Lane

N

| 0 | ¼ | ½ mile |
| 0 | ¼ | ½ kilometre |

Carter's Hill Farm from Barretts Lane.

Barkham Church and The Coombes

distance 4 mile

This circular walk, of about 4 miles in length, almost entirely in the parish of Barkham, is through the pleasant gently undulating farmland and woodland just to the south-west of Wokingham. In winter and after wet weather, some of the paths in The Coombes can be rather muddy, so do go suitably shod.

The directions below start from the east end of Coombes Lane, at its junction with Bearwood Road (Grid Ref. 783678), but the map of the route may suggest other starting places. For further topo-graphical features of the area, see the Ordnance Survey Pathfinder map 1188 'Mortimer and Arborfield'. Please observe the Country Code; in particular, keep to footpaths, keep dogs on lead across farmland and leave all wild flowers for others to enjoy.

From the end of Coombes Lane, cross Bearwood Road and continue along Sandy Lane, tarmac at first, then narrow path after concrete posts. Follow right-hand bend in lane just after three white houses on right. At crossroads ahead, turn right along road (B3349) and about halfway down Doles Hill, immediately before property 356A, turn left along gravel track. When track bends left, continue straight on over stile with fence on left and ditch on right. After further stile at road ahead, cross over road to enter path opposite, between fence on left and buildings on right.

After stile into field ahead, bear slightly right through middle of field to stile in far boundary, here cross over farm track (Nashgrove Ride) and then bridge over Barkham Brook. After stile next to metal gate, keep straight on through middle of field ahead and after further stile, continue along edge of next field with hedge on left in direction of spire to - Barkham Church. Enter churchyard through gap in fence to pass the stone and flint-faced St. James's Church on right, then continue past pond on left along Church Lane ahead.

At road junction, cross over and turn right along footway, then immediately before 'The White Cottage' on left, turn left into fenced and hedged path, and after stile enter narrow field ahead. Shortly join farm track and after crossin ditch, continue along edge of next field with ditch and fence on left. After stile ahead, continue in field with hedge on left, then just beyond red brick cottage, climb stile on left to follow fenced grave track. At Barkham Road (B3349) ahead, with care cross over to footway opposit and turn right along road, then about 70 yards after crossing bridge over Barkham Brook, turn left up broad grave track. Keep to right of gateway to Rectory and after passing buildings immediately on left, continue on climbing woodland path to enter - The Coombes.

Just before grass clearing ahead (by large chestnut tree) turn left on waymarked (painted white arrows) woodland path to shortly cross deep hollow via steps and footbridge. At far side of hollow bear left for a few yards and then right, down slope, to soon follow raised path. After about 150 yards switch to other side of bank. At path junction, at near corner of field on left, continue straight on over wooden footbridge keeping field nearby or adja-cent on left. At end of field pass throug tall stileway, then climb steeply throug tall conifers ahead and at path junction at top of rise (Gravelpit Hill) turn right along broad woodland track (Coombes Lane) - here shortly observe through trees on left, the distant red brick Bearwood College, the Royal Merchant Navy School. On reaching near corner of field on right, keep straight on along broad fenced path to return to start.

DATE WALKED [| | 19   ]

Ramble No. 20

In the Coombes

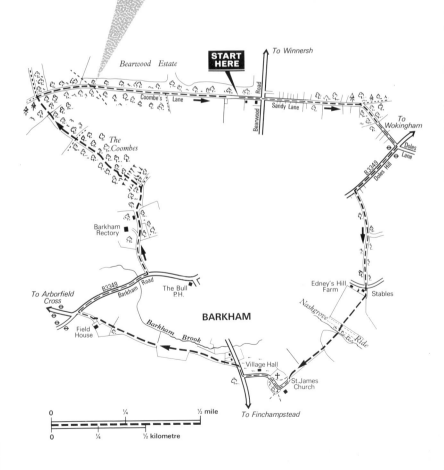

To Winnersh

START HERE

Bearwood Estate

Coombe's Lane

Bearwood Road

Sandy Lane

To Wokingham

Doles Lane

The Coombes

B3349

Doles Hill

Barkham Rectory

Edney's Hill Farm

Stables

The Bull P.H.

Nashgrove Ride

To Arborfield Cross

B3349 Barkham Road

BARKHAM

Field House

Barkham Brook

Village Hall

St. James Church

To Finchampstead

0	¼	½ mile

| 0 | ¼ | ½ kilometre |

Burghfield Lock and Calcot Mill

distance 3½ miles

This circular walk, of about 3½ miles, while just on the fringe of urban Reading, meanders through beautiful meadows bordering the Holy Brook and the River Kennet, and visits the centuries-old Calcot Mill. Before long we hope it will be possible to avoid the stretch of Burghfield Road by using the longer circuit via Milkmaids Bridge, as the map shows. Although local people may have been following the bank of the Holy Brook for many years, not all of it is a public right-of-way.

The directions below start from the car park off Brunel Road, Southcote (sign-posted 'Southcote Linear Park'. Grid Ref. 686715). For further topographical features, see the Ordnance Survey Pathfinder map 1172 'Reading'. Please observe the Country Code.

Leave car park through wooden swing-gate and turn right along well defined path. Shortly, pass through two more swing-gates and continue ahead along bank of Holy Brook. The lower part of the bridge soon ahead was built to carry the Burghfield road over only the stream but had to be raised later to span the railway. Follow the path up the bridge slope then carefully cross road and turn left over bridge to face oncoming traffic. The unpleasantness of the road will be fully compensated later!

Follow the road to just beyond the double Burghfield Bridge (over the Kennet, then the canal). Cross road at traffic lights, turn left into short track, then left again along canal towpath. This bridge was built in the early 1800s by canal engineer John Rennie, replacing an earlier swing-bridge. We are now following the Kennet Navigation, first opened in 1723, linking Reading to Newbury. In 1810 it became part of the 87-mile long Kennet & Avon Canal, to Bristol via Bath. The canal flourished until the railways came in the mid 1800s and by the 1950s was more or less derelict. In 1962 a Trust was formed by local enthusiasts to start restoration work. HM the Queen re-opened the canal in 1990. Today, the

British Waterways Board manages the canal, with financial help from the Trust and local authorities.

Follow canal bank past the 'Cunning Man' to reach and turn right over foot-bridge (Swans Bridge), designed for barge horses to cross. Along here are the remains of osier beds which provided willow for basket making. Soon arrive at Burghfield Lock, which seems far from the madding crowd. It is interesting to try to 'spot the joins' between the Kennet river and the specially made 'cuts', on one of which this lock stands.

From the lock continue along the bank. A stile followed by a wide, raised embankment marks the beginning of a stretch of the old River Kennet. Follow its meanderings to the end of a meadow at Hissey's Bridge. Instead of crossing the stile ahead, turn sharp right, still in the field, and head towards a white painted stile to left of power line posts. Carefully cross two stiles and railway line between, before turning right to follow the bank again of the now familiar Holy Brook. Without crossing it, go 30 yards beyond footbridge over stream, then bear right across middle of field to far corner and continue along tree-lined track with ditch, then stream,

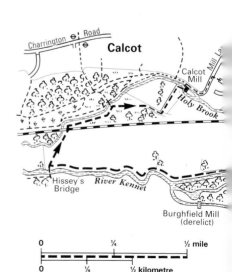

Ramble No. 21

Near Burghfield Lock

on left. Turn left over concrete foot-bridge and go straight across field ahead with wire fence on left. A concrete track leads over mill stream. Turn right between the buildings of Calcot Mill. This mill was once part of the manor of Tilehurst (today in Theale parish) and was held by the monks until Henry VIII dissolved Reading Abbey. Queen Elizabeth I may not have slept here but in 1593 she certainly leased 'a mill at Tilehurst' to her favourite, Robert, Earl of Essex. A working mill until about 1964, it was later largely destroyed by fire. The original stone walls and the still turning water-wheel today form part of the garden alongside the converted Granary. Notice also the Coach-house and 18th century one-time miller's house.

From the mill follow the gravel drive (a public path) leading onto a road. At top of slope turn right on tarmac path between garden fences. Continue ahead through bends of an estate road (Hawkesbury Drive). At No. 41 (on right), bear right for 50 yards, then turn sharp right to enter grass area through swing-gate. Turn left along well defined path with hedge and railway on right. This pleasant broad grassland strip,, leads us back in 3/4 mile to Burghfield Road crossing and the start.

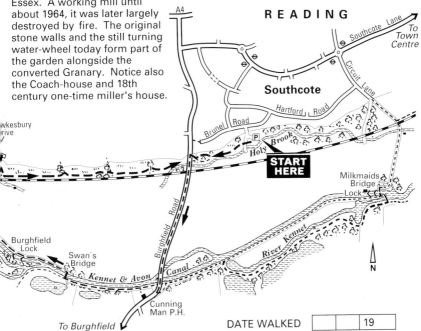

DATE WALKED | | 19 |

Spencers Wood and Priory Farm

This fairly level circular walk, of about 5 miles, covers a variety of scenery, fields, farms and woodland to the south of the village of Spencers Wood. In winter and after wet weather Beech Hill Covert can be muddy, so do go suitably shod.

The directions below start from the Basingstoke Road, just south of the junction with Hyde End Road (B3349) (Grid Ref. 715666). Buses stop here and cars can be parked on the verge opposite shops and houses. For further topographical features of the area see the Ordnance Survey Pathfinder map 1188 'Mortimer and Arborfield'. Please observe the Country Code.

Cross over the Basingstoke Road into Spring Gardens and shortly join tarmac path-way leading to estate road (Larchside Close). Just beyond No. 1 (on right) turn left beside wooden 5-bar gate and follow grassy tree-lined footpath. On reaching roadside (Hyde End Road) turn right along foot-way for 1/4 mile, to take first turning on right, Sussex Lane, which soon becomes a gravel road-way with variety of property. Cross stile beside metal gate ahead to cross fields ahead (which appear to have been 'set-aside' long before the current phrase came into use!)

On far side turn right over stile (hidden by bush!) and follow shallow ditch at first, between open fields. Soon bear left alongside a concreted area (currently used as a silage clamp). Facing open field turn left on gravel track alongside trees to pass farm buildings on right and then, on left, the moated Sheepbridge Court. Carefully cross road and continue straight ahead on wide grass track. Entering field ahead between wooden posts, turn left to follow field edge with hedge and trees on left almost hiding the River Loddon. Cross plank footbridge and stile and follow right-hand boundary of meadow to reach stile at road.

Turn right along lane then left at T junction, passing property 'Kingsbridge' on left At end of trees on left turn sharp left

on track to pass under dual carriageway and on the far side turn right up slope. At end of woodland on left, turn left over stile. On left is a copse surrounded by the remains of a moat, known as Beaumys Castle. In 1339, the Lord of the Manor, Nicholas de la Beche (whose family gave its name to the village of Beech Hill), obtained a licence from the king to crenellate (fortify) his house. Perhaps it stood here.

Follow edge of field to cross footbridge and stile ahead then bear slightly left on definitive path towards a point between buildings of Priory Farm. Stay on same line over concrete yard ahead. Over fence on left can be seen the back of a very old house, known today as The Priory which in its idyllic Loddon-side setting was painted by John Constable in 1821. The earliest building on this site was the 12th century Hermitage of St. Leonard, later converted to a private house which for nearly 500 years until 1924, belonged to Eton College. It is surely one of Berkshire's most historic houses.

When level with Priory Farmhouse look left to see a well preserved granary on staddle stones. Leaving farmyard, turn right along tarmac drive to lodge. Here turn right along road (Wood Lane), pass through stileway and continue along bridleway with woodland both sides. Where lane turns right go ahead over new bridleway bridge, then bear left through woodland. On reaching road (Beech Hill Road) opposite Brook Farm, turn right along grass verge and over by-pass. Here cross to left-hand side of road to follow path alongside fence. At top of rise bear left along lane with wide views across countryside. Go straight on at crossing lane and over stile by rusty gate.

In wood keep field close by on right to cross footbridge followed by stile. Turn right for 50 yards along a track (Kit Lane), then left over stile to follow field fence back to Basingstoke Road and the start.

DATE WALKED [   ] [19]

Ramble No. 22

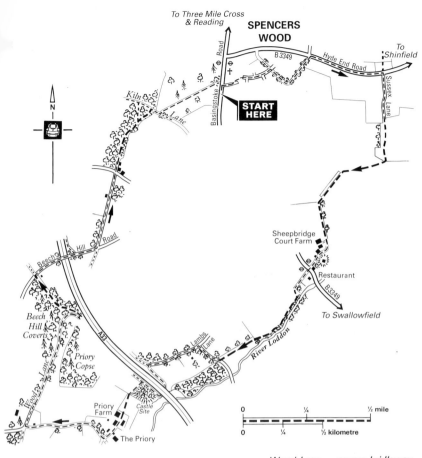

To Three Mile Cross & Reading

SPENCERS WOOD

To Shinfield

B.3349

Hyde End Road

Sussex Lane

Basingstoke Road

Kiln Lane

START HERE

Sheepbridge Court Farm

Restaurant

B.3349

To Swallowfield

Beech Hill Road

Beech Hill Coverts

Priory Copse

Wood Lane

Priory Farm

Castle Site

The Priory

Lambs Lane

River Loddon

| 0 | ¼ | ½ mile |
| 0 | ¼ | ½ kilometre |

Wood Lane ~ now a bridleway

Hurst Village and River Loddon

This circular walk, of just over 4 miles, passes through the largely unspoilt village of Hurst and its surrounding meadows, returning along the banks of the River Loddon on a new path created in 1991 - a 'planning gain' from nearby gravel extraction.

The directions below start from the car park in Sandford Lane (Grid ref. 787727) opposite Black Swan Sailing Club. For further topographical features see the O.S. Pathfinder map 1172 'Reading'. Please observe the Country Code.

From the car park entrance, turn left along the lane past Park Cottage and follow grass verge. Outside the gates of Hurst Grove turn right and shortly cross with care into Dunt Lane for a few yards before turning left over stile. Cross this large meadow, divided by wire fences, aiming to left of farm buildings (Hatch Gate Fm.), to reach a stile onto footbridge. Go straight ahead along road for 100 yards before bearing left into short track, with hedge on left, to enter pasture ahead at stile by gate. Take diagonal line up towards top corner of field, with glimpse of church tower ahead through trees.

Cross stile and turn right up lane. The Church of St. Nicholas dates from the 12th century; the tower was built in 1612, the south side and porch were added in 1875. The Almshouses on our right were built in 1682 as a 'Hospital for the maintenance of 8 poor persons at 6d per diem (day) for ever.' Inflation had not been discovered! Further along stands the Castle inn, still with a bowling green said to have been laid in 1628 for the benefit of Charles I.

As an alternative to following the road past the Castle, we can take the gravel path leading behind the church, where you may catch sight of Hurst House through an avenue of trees, a manor first built in 1530 and largely rebuilt in 1847 after a fire. Follow path bearing left into graveyard to reach the road. Here turn left, along right-hand side of the road. Just beyond Old School House turn right into Orchard Road and at end of field on left, turn left through two wooden swing-gates to reach stile into School Road. Turn right passing the infants' school (built 1843), crossing to left-hand footwa leading to village pond. Cross road junction into Hinton Road continuing on left-hand footway to reach the Green Man.

Immediately opposite the pub cross stile to take path through middle of paddock t reach stile at roadside. Cross lane and stile ahead to follow field-edge path with hedge on right. At end of field rejoin lane passing Little Farm. Keep left of thatched cottage ahead to enter a 'green lane' (Hogmore Lane). At first field entrance or left cross footbridge/stile, turning right to follow hedge theough two fields, to reach road at Broadwater Cottages.

Carefully cross busy road (A321) and stile ahead. The path here has been diverted in places, but will be restored to the correct line when gravel working has finished. At a wide 'haul route' bear left into narrow path to reach lane in 50 yards. Just to the right stands the pretty Whistley Bridge House - well worth a look - which gives us our first view of the River Loddon. Domesday Book records a mill at Whistley, valued at '5 shillings and 250 eels'. For our walk we turn left on reaching the lane for some 100 yards. An old oak on right marks a swing-gate at the start of a new path that we follow along the Loddon for just over a mile. On the left along here once stood an old manor house, Whistley Court, pulled down in the mid 1800s. Can you find any traces of the cutting from the river which once led to its thatched boathouse?

Eventually, cross a modern footbridge over the Emm Brook onto a gravel path. Where this joins a rough tarmac path look back left to see 'Teal' hide, one of two hides overlooking Lavells Lake, excellent spots for watching the wildlife, including foxes! In front of swing-gate turn sharp left on broad grass track which soon follows hedgerow on right. Follow lakeside to visit second hide or go straight on to turn left over stile at roadside to return to start.

DATE WALKED [   ] [19   ]

Ramble No. 23

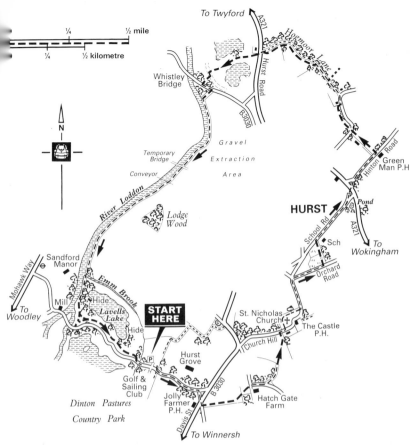

Footbridge at the mouth of the Emm Brook

Broadmoor Lane and Sonning Village

distance 3 miles

This walk, of about 3 miles, features the unspoilt historic village of Sonning, passes through the fields of Sonning Farm, returning along a peaceful stretch of the Thames riverside path above St. Patrick's Stream. A circular walk in Sonning has only been possible since the University of Reading kindly agreed in 1991 to the creation of a 'permitted path' across their land at Sonning Farm.

The directions below start from Sonning Lane (B4446) where it reaches the old part of the village (Grid ref. 756754) but the map of the route may suggest other starting places. For further topographical features of the area, see the Ordnance Survey Pathfinder map 1172 'Reading'. Please observe the Country Code.

With your back to the impressive gateway of Bishops Close (North Lodge) join the footway ahead, in front of 'Turpins' (Dick's aunt lived here). Stretching ahead on either side (Pearson Road) is surely the quintessential architecture of an English village; the art and craftsmanship of more than five centuries, timber framed cottages, elegant Georgian facades and handsome Victorian brickwork, all in complete harmony, without the help of any 'planners'!

Just before the end of Pearson Road, cross Pound Lane on right and then bear right into Charvil Lane. Where footway on right ends, with great care continue along the road for some 125 yards before turning left across the road opposite the entrance to Sonning Farm. The metal farm-gate ahead marks the beginning of what is shown on old maps as Broadmoor Lane. It is now a 'permitted path', following a suggestion made by East Berks R A Group. This is the effective answer for the landowner who welcomes walkers in the countryside but prefers not to establish a right-of-way across his land.

Follow the farm track ahead, concrete at first, then gravel, slowly descending with open views. On reaching farmbuildings on right, go straight ahead along grassy track, to leave the fields by wooden swing-gate. Turn left along tarmac lane (Milestone Avenue) to soon reach metal road-bridge over St. Patrick's Stream. A right-of-way continues ahead here, leading eventually to Wargrave, but our route turns left immediately before the bridge shortly to join the riverbank. The towpath (newly designated as The Thames Path) is on the far bank, making this one of the all too rare stretches where one can walk for any distance along both sides of the

The Bull at Sonning

Ramble No. 24